THE COURTROOM TRIAL of Jesus the Christ

A Legal Study of the Gospel of John

By Dr. Jimmy F. Orr

Foreword by B. Phillip Bettis

ISBN-13: 978-1512053401
ISBN-10: 1512053406

Dedication

This book is dedicated to…

… my wife and best friend, Amanda;

… my talented son, Zach, and his wonderful wife, Micole;

… my beautiful daughter, Hillary;

… and to the gracious people at Palmetto Baptist Church, Palmetto, Georgia, who have kept coming for fifteen years to hear my sermons.

Table of Contents

Acknowledgements

In writing and editing this book, I had the help of a lot of people. This book originated as a series of sermons preached in 2011 at Palmetto Baptist Church, Palmetto, Georgia. I owe this great church more than I will ever be able to repay.

I want to thank my students at the Brewton-Parker College, Newnan, Georgia Campus, and at the Frederick M. Hawkins Center for Christian Studies, Cumming, Georgia, for challenging me to never stop studying.

Special thanks go out to my wonderful friends---Judy Baird, Louise Davis, Jill Exner, Richard and Virginia Munn, Sarah Russell, Zach Orr, and my Mom, Dolores Orr, for carrying me through multiple drafts of proof-reading and corrections. Without their help, this book would have never made it to print.

Thanks to Judge Phill Bettis for writing the foreword and for his invaluable insight and recommended changes that made this book better than it ever could have been.

Thanks to my son, Zach, for the cover design.

Finally, I thank my wife, Amanda, for 31 years of her love, support, tolerance, patience, and perseverance.

Jimmy F. Orr,
Palmetto, Georgia
June 2015

“What shall I do then with Jesus who is called the Christ?”

-Pontius Pilate (Matthew 27:22)

Foreword

Jesus is on trial at this very moment! Some may question how the Son of God, who was tried almost two thousand years ago, who submitted Himself to the cruelty of crucifixion as a willing sacrifice, and who was resurrected victorious on the third day, can be tried again? As recent events and studies reveal, a very real and contemporary trial is underway with judges and jurors all around.

A little over a year ago I was asked by a dear friend, a friend who happened to be a chief judge, what I would think of becoming a part time judge. With a busy law practice, I was at first skeptical. Did I have time? What if I didn't like it? Even after practicing law for 35 years, I lacked confidence. Did I know enough about trials, evidence and the law? After much prayer and encouragement from family and friends, I decided to undertake the great honor of serving my community as a judge. I took the bench for the first time with a borrowed robe and with butterflies in my stomach.

Judging civil and criminal cases requires that decisions be made - something that rarely comes easily. Decisions in the courtroom or life affect us profoundly. I have attempted to analyze my courtroom decision making methods and in the process realized that outcomes often turn on the slightest bit of evidence or testimony. Those outcomes often result in controversy, appeals, anger, relief, and vindication. Some of those decisions will resonate in lives for decades to come.

Court is by necessity solemn and conclusory. Court is also a battleground where litigants bring a jumbled mix of facts, emotions, and indigence which are then presented to a finder of law and fact. We expect reasoned and fair outcomes discerned from what is quite often a form of managed chaos. It is amazing that court works as well as it does. Questions must be asked and answered. One axiom taught to young trial lawyers is to never ever ask a question to which you do not know the answer. There are many great lawyer stories about questions and answers changing the course of trials, especially involving questions which should have never been asked. Many of those questions and answers came as great surprises. Oddly, some questions have no answer.

In his book, ***The Courtroom Trial of Jesus the Christ***, my longtime friend and longtime pastor, Jimmy Orr has in one manner asked a question that has no earthly answer. Simply put, why would the Son of God give himself as a willing sacrifice for our sins? Our typical answers are grace and love, but what does that mean? Are those sufficient answers? How does a world short on love understand Christ's willingness to die for someone like me who did not exist until nearly two thousand years later and who is fully undeserving of such love? How do we explain our Heavenly Father planning reconciliation from the foundation of the world?

Most of us are content to ask nothing more and simply accept or reject why Christ came into the world. Dr. Orr is not so content. Using unique methods and drawing from the text of the Gospel of John, Dr. Orr places Christ on trial and makes the reader the jury. In that role, we must confront a risen Savior and our beliefs as well. Are we willing to stake our eternity on a witness who proposes answers that are otherworldly, that are not of our nature, and that very much surprise temporal advocates?

Dr. Orr subtly causes us to explore why recent studies indicate double digit declines in Christian belief among American citizens. As ambassadors of Christ, our ministries, our witness, our judgments, our worship, our failures, and our hypocrisies have been considered by a jury of public opinion. In many instances, we have been found wanting. In one method, Dr. Orr poses another question as to how well we represent our Savior. With opinions that we as Christians are harsh, judgmental, and often out of touch, one may be challenged to choose sides. Do we abide in Christ and his teachings or are we succumbing to mounting pluralistic pressures?

The Courtroom Trial of Jesus the Christ portrays with great love the Lord's example and strength during a time of trial. Through Jimmy Orr's writing, we judge ourselves, we prepare, we model, and we await the One who we will someday see face to face. For one, I am at great peace knowing that the greatest advocate in the universe sits at the right hand of my Heavenly Father making intercessions despite our questions and our incessant desire to know more about his complex, loving and graceful nature.

-B. Phillip Bettis
June 2015

Introduction

When Evelyn Bagby entered her apartment on September 21, 1957, she had no idea that she was being watched by someone who had been inside her residence while she was away. It was late. The red-headed, blue-eyed, and attractive Bagby had returned home from an evening of shopping after finishing her shift working as a waitress at the Crowncrest Tavern. In her apartment, Bagby proceeded to her bedroom, where she reached for a cigarette case inside her bureau drawer, but instead discovered a snub-nosed .38 caliber Colt revolver that did not belong to her. Her first thought was to call her attorney, Perry Mason, which she did. The call went to an answering service which, fortunately for Bagby, routed her call to Mason's office, where Mason was working at a late hour. Mason had come to Bagby's aid in an earlier case in which the woman was accused of stealing jewelry from movie star Helene Chaney at a motel in Riverside, California. Mason's team successfully defended Bagby, convincing the jury that someone had set her up.

On the phone, Bagby told Mason that she had found a gun in her apartment. Mason explained how to check whether the gun had been fired. It had not. Mason then told her to leave with the gun, check into a hotel, and come to his office the next morning. Bagby left her apartment as Mason had instructed, but afterward noticed in her rearview mirror a man wearing a pillowcase hood following her. When the hooded man tried to force her off the road, Bagby pulled out the revolver and fired at the car, which swerved off the road. When Bagby reached a phone, she made a desperate call to Mason, convinced that someone had tried to murder her. Mason drove to the area where Bagby's encounter with the hooded man occurred, only to find that the Los Angeles Police Department homicide detectives were already at the scene, recovering a car that had gone over the side of a mountain. Inside the car was the body of Harry Merrill, a drama coach who at one time claimed he could get Bagby a part in a movie, then took her money and disappeared with it. Police found Merrill with a bullet in his body and a pillowcase over his head. Evelyn Bagby denied murdering Merrill, insisting she had only fired two shots to scare off a hooded man who was following her. However, she would soon be arrested for murder.

When I was growing up, the courtroom drama *Perry Mason* was among the most popular shows on television. One of the few black-and-white, hour-long series to flourish in syndication well into the twenty-first century, *Perry Mason* was the creation of Erle Stanley Gardner, a lawyer turned novelist, who introduced the character in 1933. *Perry Mason* dramas involved mysteries built around the idea of a brilliant, meticulous lawyer with sharply-honed observational and rhetorical skills, who never lost a case. The series starred Canadian actor Raymond Burr as Mason and made its CBS debut on September 21, 1957, running from 1957 to 1966.

The first episode of *Perry Mason* was "The Case of the Restless Redhead," based on Gardner's 1954 novel of the same name. Mason's client at the time was Evelyn Bagby, charged with shooting a man to death. With the odds stacked against her, Bagby needed Perry Mason to clear her name. Mason took the case and, in the end, convinced the jury to find her not guilty.

The New Testament Gospel of John reads like a courtroom trial. The author, presumably the Apostle John, wrote to make the case for Jesus Christ. As in Perry Mason's case on behalf of Evelyn Bagby, the odds were stacked against him. First, John wrote toward the end of the first century when the Roman Empire demonstrated periodic hostility toward Christians. This made the act of recording Jesus' ministry a dangerous endeavor. Second, John wrote a narrative replete with miraculous events that most people did not believe possible. John was vulnerable to criticism and even persecution for reporting that Jesus had performed such miracles.

Although John was a fisherman, not a lawyer, he utilized some of the same strategies used by an attorney in a courtroom trial. First, trial attorneys develop a theme for the trial. Second, attorneys make opening statements. Third, they call witnesses to testify. Fourth, they present physical evidence to support their cases, often reserving the most compelling piece of physical evidence for last. Fifth, a trial lawyer may call expert witnesses to testify. Sixth, persons of great reputation in the community might be called as character witnesses. Seventh, lawyers cross-examine prosecution witnesses, as well as prepare their own defendants for cross-examination. Eighth, a lawyer might put the defendant on the stand. And finally, attorneys often rely on historical precedent to plead their cases.

What we discover in the Gospel of John is that John utilized all of these legal strategies to plead his case for Jesus. We do not have to be Bible scholars to find these strategies; John places them clearly throughout his Gospel. *The purpose of this book is to show John's use of legal strategies in making his case for Jesus.*

1 Pre-Trial Preparation

Overview of the Gospel of John

Before proceeding with the legal strategy of John, we must conduct some pre-trial preparation by considering the background of John's Gospel. Examining the background of a New Testament book requires answering the following questions about that book: Who was the author? When was the book written? What time period did the author of the book describe? Who were the first readers of the book? What is the general content of the book? What are the major emphases of the author? What special characteristics are found in the book? In addition to these questions, we will examine the Gospel of John to determine who the prosecution in this case could be.

Who Was the Author?

The Gospel of John, like Matthew, Mark, and Luke, is anonymous; it does not bear the name of its author. The title 'According to John' was attached when the Gospels were compiled and circulated as a single collection during the late second century. The titles were added to distinguish each Gospel from the others. Most traditional scholars, such as F.F. Bruce[1] and Leon Morris[2], contend that the beloved disciple who "wrote these things down" (John 21:24; 13:23; 19:25-27; 20:2; 21:7) refers to John the Apostle, son of Zebedee. These scholars point to passages such as John 21:20-24.

> Peter turned and saw that the disciple whom Jesus loved was following them. (This was the one who had leaned back

[1] Bruce, F.F. *The Gospel of John: Introduction, Exposition, Notes*. Wm. B. Eerdmans Publishing, Jan 1, 1994.

[2] Morris, Leon. The Gospel According to John. Wm. B. Eerdmans Publishing, 1995.

> against Jesus at the supper and had said, "Lord, who is going to betray you?") When Peter saw him, he asked, "Lord, what about him?" Jesus answered, "If I want him to remain alive until I return, what is that to you? You must follow me." Because of this, the rumor spread among the believers that this disciple would not die. But Jesus did not say that he would not die; he only said, "If I want him to remain alive until I return, what is that to you?" *This is the disciple who testifies to these things and who wrote them down. We know that his testimony is true.*[3]

Most scholars agree that the final chapter of John's Gospel was added later, and that the "we" of John 21:24 suggests that other persons are responsible for John's Gospel in its final form.[4] Many contemporary scholars believe that a different person familiar with John authored the entire fourth Gospel. Princeton theologian James Charlesworth says the Apostle Thomas wrote John's Gospel. Methodist scholar Ben Witherington believes the author was Lazarus.[5] And author Esther de Boer suggests that the author of John's Gospel was Mary Magdalene.[6]

Others believe the author was a committee of unknown authors and editors—the Johannine community. The liberal theologian John Shelby Spong says:

> There is no way that the Fourth Gospel was written by John Zebedee or by any of the disciples of Jesus. The author of this book is not a single individual, but is at least three different writers/editors, who did their layered work over a period of 25 to 30 years.[7]

From the text, we can derive at least three facts concerning the author. First, the author was Jewish or at least intimately familiar with Jewish literature and culture. He quoted occasionally from the Hebrew text of the Old Testament (John 12:40; 13:18; 19:37); he was acquainted with the

---

[3] John 21:20-24.

[4] Fee, Gordon D. and Douglas Stuart. *How to Read the Bible Book by Book: A Guided Tour.* Zondervan Publishing, March 18, 2002.

[5] http://benwitherington.blogspot.com/2007/01/was-lazarus-beloved-disciple.html.

[6] http://www.bloomsbury.com/us/the-gospel-of-mary-9780826480019/.

[7] http://www.huffingtonpost.com/john-shelby-spong/gospel-of-john-what-everyone-knows-about-the-fourth-gospel_b_3422026.html

Jewish feasts such as the Passover (John 2:13; 5:1; 6:4; 11:55), Tabernacles (John 7:37), and Dedication/Hanukkah (John 10:22); and he was familiar with Jewish customs such as the arranging of water pots (John 2) and burial customs (John 11:38-44). Second, the author had firsthand knowledge of Palestine. He knew that Jacob's well was deep (John 4:11); he described a descent from Canaan to Capernaum; and he distinguished between Bethany and Bethany beyond the Jordan; in short, he was intimately acquainted with Palestinian topography. Third, the author was either an eyewitness or was acquainted with someone who witnessed the events he portrayed. He stated that he beheld Christ's glory (John 1:14), using a verb which in New Testament Greek most often bore the meaning of at least physical examination. The author made incidental comments about his being among Jesus' followers at certain events in Jesus' life, showing intimate knowledge of what happened among the disciples (Judas slipped out at night [John 13:30]; Jesus was tired at Jacob's Well [John 4:6]; the disciples were frightened on a boat [John 6:19]). The writer was exact in mentioning names of characters present at various points in the book.

When Was the Book Written?

When considering the dating of New Testament books, one must consider both the date in which the book was written as well as the time period the book describes. As to when the Gospel of John was written, scholars disagree, with some contending that it was written in the middle of the first century, and others holding that John wrote late in the first century, around 90-100 C.E. The earliest fragment of any New Testament book is of a portion of the Gospel of John, dating back to about 125 C.E. This small manuscript was written in Greek, with words on the front and back. The front contains parts of seven lines from John 18:31–33, and the back consists of parts of seven lines from verses 37–38. The existence of this fragment suggests that the Gospel of John was written sometime in the first century. Almost all scholars believe that John's Gospel was the last of the four Gospels to be written. Mark's Gospel was written first, sometime during the 60s C.E. Matthew and Luke most likely were written in the 70s or 80s C.E. That John outlines a more mature view of Jesus (Christology[8])

[8] Christology is the study of the person of Jesus Christ.

than the Synoptic Gospels[9] suggests that the Gospel of John was written later in the first century, perhaps the late 80s or 90s C.E.

What Time Period Did the Author of the Book Describe?

With the exception of the opening lines which locate Jesus with God in eternity in the past, John's Gospel recorded the life and ministry of Jesus. Therefore, we can safely assume that the time period John depicted was early in the first century since Jesus lived during that time. Because John omitted the story of the birth of Christ and focused primarily on the life and ministry of Christ, we can further narrow the time period John described to 25-35 C.E. This dating assumes Jesus was born around 6 B.C.E. since King Herod, who tried to kill the baby Jesus, died in 4 B.C.E. Herod died not long after the slaughter of the infant boys in Bethlehem (Matthew 2:16-18), which took place before Jesus turned two years of age. The dating also assumes that Jesus started his ministry around age 30, according to Luke 3:23. In addition, Pontius Pilate, the procurator at the time of Jesus' crucifixion, served as the Roman Prefect in Judea from 26-36 C.E. Jesus would have turned thirty in 24 C.E., putting the end of his ministry squarely within Pilate's term. Although there is much debate as to the actual date of Jesus' death, my own view is that Jesus was crucified at Passover during the year 30 C.E., the only year during Pilate's administration when Passover fell on a Friday. Thus, John's Gospel focused on a narrow time period in Palestine dated roughly 26-30 C.E.

Who Were the First Readers of the Book?

The recipients are traditionally thought to have been a Christian community located in or around the city of Ephesus, in what is now Turkey. Tradition holds that John ministered in the area of Ephesus later in his life, and was afterward arrested by the Romans under the Emperor Domitian, who exiled him to the Island of Patmos. That the recipients were largely Gentile[10] is seen by the references to Jews as the enemies of Christ, as well as by the many explanations and interpretations that would have been unnecessary had John written to a Jewish audience (John 1:38, 41, 42; 5:2, et. al.). For instance, in John 1:38, John portrayed Jesus responding to the curiosity of

---

[9] Synoptic Gospels is the term used to denote the Gospels of Matthew, Mark, and Luke.

[10] Non-Jewish.

the followers of John the Baptizer. When the Baptizer's followers addressed Jesus as "Rabbi," the author inserted a parenthetical synonym for 'Rabbi' which would not have been necessary had John's readers been Jewish.

> Turning around, Jesus saw them following and asked, "What do you want?"
> They said, "Rabbi" *(which means "Teacher")*, "where are you staying?"[11]

What Is the General Content of John's Gospel?

John's Gospel contains the story of the life, ministry, and death of Jesus, the Messiah and Son of God, and the implications of that story for humankind. According to John, Jesus had always existed co-eternally with God the Father and was always equal to God in nature. John taught that Jesus, in his incarnation, made God known and made his life available to all humanity through the cross. John, more than any other Gospels, emphasized the deity of Jesus. Not only did he say that Jesus was with God from the beginning, but he also contended that Jesus was God. John's Jesus was responsible for creation, was crucified as "the Lamb of God who takes away the sin of the world" (John 1:29), and rose from the dead as the true conqueror of death. John affirmed that Jesus was the long-awaited Messiah, fulfilling every Jewish expectation and hope for what and who the Messiah was supposed to be. Most importantly, John presented Jesus as the source of eternal life. John communicated all of this in hopes that his readers would make a decision to follow Christ.

What Are the Major Emphases of John's Gospel?

The major emphases in John's Gospel revolve around the Godhead: the Father, the Son, and the Holy Spirit. God the Father is the eternal divine being who created the universe and is sovereign over all creation. Jesus is the Messiah, the Son of God. In his incarnation and the crucifixion, Jesus both revealed God's love and redeemed humanity. In John's Gospel, following Jesus meant to "remain in the vine," who was Jesus, and to bear fruit in Jesus' name (John 15). The Holy Spirit was given to people in order to empower them to continue Jesus' work (John 15:26-27).

---

[11] John 1:38.

What Are Some Special Characteristics of the Gospel of John?

The Gospel of John is noticeably different from Matthew, Mark, and Luke. John showed Jesus predominantly in Jerusalem, whereas the Synoptic Gospels located Jesus primarily in Galilee. John's Gospel contains no Messianic Secret, referring to the phenomenon, mainly found in the Gospel of Mark, in which Jesus commanded his followers not to reveal who he was after he performed certain miracles. According to John, Jesus' public ministry extended over a period of at least three and possibly four years, based upon the number of times John mentioned the annual Passover Feast. During this time, Jesus made several journeys from Galilee to Jerusalem. On the other hand, Matthew, Mark, and Luke mentioned only one journey of Jesus to Jerusalem (the final one), with most of Jesus' ministry taking place in Galilee within the space of what appears to be only one year.

John left out many of the most familiar events in Jesus' life described by the Synoptic writers. Among the more surprising omissions by John are the temptation of Jesus, his transfiguration, and the institution of the Lord's Supper. John mentioned no examples of Jesus casting out demons. The Sermon on the Mount and the Lord's Prayer are not found in the fourth Gospel. In addition, John did not include the narrative parables such as the ones found especially in Luke. Most scholars view John 15:1-8 "the Vine and the Branches" as an analogy rather than a parable.

But John did include material not found in the other Gospels. Almost none of the material in John 2-4, which consists of Jesus' early Galilean ministry, is found in the other Gospels. The resurrection of Lazarus (John 11) surprisingly is not mentioned in the Synoptic Gospels, though certainly Matthew, Mark, and Luke would have known about it. Jesus' "I Am" statements (The Good Shepherd, The Vine, The Bread of Life, The Door, The Way, The Truth, The Life, etc.), of which there are nine in John, are not found in the other Gospels at all. These "I Am" statements allude to Exodus 3:14 and point to Jesus' deity (John 8:24, 28, 58). John began his Gospel with eternity past ("In the beginning the Word already was…"), whereas Mark began his Gospel with Jesus' baptism, and Matthew and Luke began their Gospels with Jesus' birth. The extended Farewell Discourse (John 13-17) is not found in any other Gospel. The teaching discourses in John are long rather than short condensed statements found in the Synoptics (with the notable exception of the Sermon on the Mount in Matthew 5-7).

In his Gospel, John often used terms that have double meanings or stories with double meanings. Therefore, understanding the fourth Gospel is like peeling an onion: one layer of meaning opens up to reveal another meaning. John made more frequent use of these literary techniques than did the other Gospel writers. Examples of these techniques can be found in John 2:25 (temple/body); John 7:37-38 (water/spirit); and John 12:32 (lifted up/exalted). W. Hall Harris III, Professor of New Testament Studies at Dallas Theological Seminary, notes that much of this symbolism takes the form of dualistic antitheses: light/darkness (John 1:4; 3:19; 8:12; 11:9; 12:35, 46); truth/falsehood (John 8:44); life/death (John 5:24; 11:25); above/below (John 8:23); and freedom/slavery (John 8:33, 36).[12]

At times it is impossible to tell with absolute certainty where Jesus stopped talking in a certain context and where John himself started interpreting (this Gospel is especially problematic for red-letter Bible editions). For instance, take the following passage from John 3.

> "You are Israel's teacher," said Jesus, "and do you not understand these things? Very truly I tell you, we speak of what we know, and we testify to what we have seen, but still you people do not accept our testimony. I have spoken to you of earthly things and you do not believe; how then will you believe if I speak of heavenly things? No one has ever gone into heaven except the one who came from heaven—the Son of Man. Just as Moses lifted up the snake in the wilderness, so the Son of Man must be lifted up, that everyone who believes may have eternal life in him."[13]
>
> For God so loved the world that he gave his one and only Son, that whoever believes in him shall not perish but have eternal life. For God did not send his Son into the world to condemn the world, but to save the world through him. Whoever believes in him is not condemned, but whoever does not believe stands condemned already because they have not believed in the name of God's one and only Son. This is the verdict: Light has come

[12] Major Differences Between John and the Synoptic Gospels - Introduction: The Relationship of John's Gospel to the Synoptics. By W. Hall Harris III, from https://bible.org/seriespage/major-differences-between-john-and-synoptic-gospels
[13] John 3:10-15

> into the world, but people loved darkness instead of light because their deeds were evil. Everyone who does evil hates the light, and will not come into the light for fear that their deeds will be exposed. But whoever lives by the truth comes into the light, so that it may be seen plainly that what they have done has been done in the sight of God.[14]

In verses 10-12, Jesus clearly was speaking. However, beginning with verse 13, it is difficult to determine when the words of Jesus stopped and the editorial of the writer began. Many red-letter versions of the New Testament begin Jesus' words at verse 10 and continue them through verse 21. But it is possible that Jesus' words ended with verse 12 after the words "how then will you believe if I speak of heavenly things?" followed by John's editorial remarks, which continued through verse 21. This would make John 3:16, the most memorized and quoted verse in Scripture, come from the pen of John rather than the lips of Jesus. Keep in mind also that in the earliest Greek manuscripts of the New Testament, there were no punctuation marks. Therefore, the quotation marks at the end of verse 15 were added by later translators and reflect the opinions of those translators.

John clearly revealed his purpose for writing at the end of his Gospel (John 20:30-31). Such a clearly stated purpose makes the study of John easier to follow (more on this later).

One other note relating to the Gospel of John concerns the story of the woman caught in adultery (John 7:53–8:11). Although this passage sounds authentic and is characteristic of what we would expect of Jesus, most likely it was not a part of the original contents of John. The earliest manuscripts do not have John 7:53—8:11. The first surviving Greek manuscript to contain the story is a Latin/Greek manuscript of the late 4th or early 5th century. A few later manuscripts incorporate these verses, wholly or in part, after John 7:36, John 21:25, Luke 21:38 or Luke 24:53.

Identifying the Prosecution in John's Gospel

The attorneys for the prosecution in this courtroom trial are derived from the forces of evil confronted in the Gospel of John. The general Christian understanding of evil is that a particular force, usually named Satan, is behind every evil event, whether moral or natural, that has ever transpired. In some books of the Bible, this underlying force is obvious, such as when

---

[14] John 3:16-21

Satan showed up in the book of Job for a celestial conference and then proceeded to coax God into allowing havoc on Job.[15] Another example of the obvious presence of evil comes when Matthew, Mark, and Luke describe Satan tempting Jesus in the desert immediately following Jesus' baptism at the hands of John the Baptizer.[16]

In John's Gospel, the force behind evil is much more subtle. John included no temptation of Jesus, and he mentioned Satan by name only once. Instead, John employed a series of words to denote the presence of evil. He made use of two Greek words, *ponera* and *phaula*, that are translated evil. He used *ponera* in three places. In John 3:19, John said, "This is the verdict: Light has come into the world, but people loved darkness instead of light because their deeds were *evil*." In John 7:7, he quoted Jesus saying, "The world cannot hate you, but it hates me because I testify that its works are *evil*." Then, in John 17:15, John described Jesus praying, "My prayer is not that you take them out of the world but that you protect them from the *evil one*."

On two occasions, John utilized the word *phaula* for evil. John 3:20 says, "Everyone who does *evil* hates the light, and will not come into the light for fear that their deeds will be exposed." John quoted Jesus in John 5:28-29, saying, "Do not be amazed at this, for a time is coming when all who are in their graves will hear his voice and come out—those who have done what is good will rise to live, and those who have done what is *evil* will rise to be condemned."

Another word John used was *kakos* which can be translated "evil" or "wrong." In John 18:23, after being struck by a servant of the High Priest, Jesus countered, "If I said something *wrong*, testify as to what is *wrong*. But if I spoke the truth, why did you strike me?" The Septuagint[17] (LXX) sometimes used this term for evil. One example of this is Isaiah 45:7, where God said, "I form the light and create darkness, I bring prosperity and create *evil*; I, the Lord, do all these things." This word in the Septuagint is the translation of the Hebrew *ra*, which is the root word used for evil throughout the Hebrew Bible.

More often, John described evil forces as "darkness," a translation of the Greek word *scotia* (pronounced sko-TEE-ya). This word occurs in five

---

[15] Job 1-2

[16] Matthew 4:1-11; Mark 1:12-13; Luke 4:1-13

[17] The Septuagint refers to the Greek translation of the Hebrew Old Testament. The translation dates between the second and third centuries BCE. The Roman abbreviation LXX is often used to refer to the Septuagint.

places in John's Gospel. In John 1:5, the author stated, "The light shines in the *darkness*, and the *darkness* has not overcome it." Again in John 3:19, he said, "This is the verdict: Light has come into the world, but people loved *darkness* instead of light because their deeds were evil." In John 8:12, Jesus said, "I am the light of the world. Whoever follows me will never walk in *darkness*, but will have the light of life." In John 12:35, Jesus stated, "You are going to have the light just a little while longer. Walk while you have the light, before *darkness* overtakes you. Whoever walks in the *dark* does not know where they are going." Jesus again in chapter 12:46 said, "I have come into the world as a light, so that no one who believes in me should stay in *darkness*."

On three occasions, John used the Greek word *diabolos* to describe the devil or to characterize another person as a devil. Referring to Judas in John 6:70, Jesus said, "Have I not chosen you, the Twelve? Yet one of you is a *devil*."

Speaking to the Pharisees in John 8:44, Jesus said:

> You belong to your father, the *devil*, and you want to carry out your father's desires. He was a murderer from the beginning, not holding to the truth, for there is no truth in him. When he lies, he speaks his native language, for he is a liar and the father of lies.[18]

Finally, in John 13:2, John described the devil as having prompted the actions of Judas Iscariot: "The evening meal was in progress, and the *devil* had already prompted Judas, the son of Simon Iscariot, to betray Jesus."

Satan himself is mentioned by name only one time in John 13:27, where it says, "As soon as Judas took the bread, *Satan* entered into him." The Greek word for Satan is *satanas*, meaning "the accuser" or "the adversary." For purposes of giving names to members of the prosecution team, we will use *shaytan*, which is the Arabic spelling of the name Satan.

A combination of these original language terms gives us the names of the prosecuting attorneys who will prosecute the case against Jesus:

Shaytan Diablo Kakos, Lead Prosecutor
Paula Ponera, Assistant Prosecutor
Ray Skotia, Assistant Prosecutor

---

[18] John 8:44

Mr. Shaytan Kakos (Satan Evil) will be the lead prosecutor, aided by Miss Paula Ponera (Evil Evil) and Mr. Ray Skotia (Evil Darkness). Throughout this text, Prosecutor Kakos will conduct most of the questioning with Assistant Prosecutor Ray Scotia questioning witnesses considered to be of lesser significance. Assistant Prosecutor Paula Ponera will question all the female witnesses.

2 John's Trial Theme

One of the most important strategy decisions an attorney makes is selecting the right theme for the trial. Consider, for instance, the case of the infamous Captain William Kidd. In the late 1600s, William Kidd (1654-1701) was a Scottish ship captain, a bounty hunter for pirates, and, later, a pirate himself. In May 1696 Kidd set sail for Madagascar and the Indian Ocean, then a hotbed of pirate activity. He intended to capture pirates and French vessels, since at the time, England was at war with France. But Kidd and his crew found few pirates or French vessels to take. About a third of his crew died of disease, and the remaining sailors became restless due to the lack of action. So Kidd turned to piracy. In August 1697 he attacked a convoy of Indian treasure ships, an act of piracy, but was driven off by an East India Company Man of War. About this time, Kidd killed a gunner named William Moore by hitting him in the head with a heavy wooden bucket. After news of Kidd's turning to piracy reached England, government officials placed a bounty on his head. When Kidd reached the Caribbean, he discovered he was being sought for piracy. He fled to New York, hoping for protection from his friends, but they turned him in to British authorities.

Kidd's trial took place on May 8, 1701, at the Old Bailey Courthouse in London, England. At the proceedings, the prosecution presented the following opening statement:

> "My Lord, and you gentlemen of the jury, this is an indictment of murder. The indictment sets forth: 'That William Kidd, on the 30th of October, on the high sea, on the coast of Malabar, did assault one William Moore on board a ship called the Adventure, whereof William Kidd was captain, struck him with a wooden bucket, hooped with iron, on the side of the head near the right ear, and that of this bruise William Moore died

> the next day, and so that William Kidd has murdered the same person.' To this indictment the defendant pleaded not guilty; if we prove him guilty, you must find him so. We will prove this as particular as can be, that William Kidd was captain of the ship, and that William Moore was under him in the ship, and that without any provocation the accused gave him the blow whereof he died. It will appear to be a most barbarous fact, to murder a man in this manner; for the man gave him no provocation. This William Moore was a gunner in the ship and this William Kidd abused him, and called him a "lousy dog," and upon a civil answer by Moore the accused took his bucket and knocked him on the head, whereof he died the next day".[19]

Captain Kidd was found guilty of Moore's murder and sentenced to death by hanging. The sentence was carried out on May 23, 1701, at the execution dock near the Tower of London. Kidd's body was put into an iron cage hanging along the River Thames, where it would serve as a warning to other pirates. The prosecutor incorporated a common trial theme of pitting the weak and innocent (William Moore) versus the powerful and corrupt (Captain William Kidd).[20]

The theme is the general storyline of the case. Lawyers choose a theme that is easily memorized, that resonates with the average person, and that motivates the jury to agree with their case.[21]

Dr. Amy Singer, a teacher and writer for *Trial Magazine*, said:

> Persuasion is a story-telling skill that depends on a clearly-defined and broadly-accepted theme to be successful - "Give me liberty or give me death," "The only thing we have to fear is fear itself," "Ask not what your country can do for you but what you can do for your country." Strong themes such as these crystallize complex concepts and arguments while at the

---

[19] Howell, Thomas Bayly, and Thomas Jones Howell. *A Complete Collection of State Trials and Proceedings for High Treason and Other Crimes and Misdemeanors from the Earliest Period to the Year 1783: 1700-08*. pp. 123-134.

[20] Defoe, Daniel (Captain Charles Johnson). *A General History of the Pyrates*. Edited by Manuel Schonhorn. Mineola: Dover Publications, 1972/1999.

[21] Gilbert, David I., Michael E. Gilfarb, Stephen K. Talpins. *Basic Trial Techniques for Prosecutors*. American Prosecutors Research Institute – Special Topics Series. p. 3. May 2005.

> same time making the ideas they represent impossible to forget and many times even impossible to deny.[22]

Singer noted that "a trial theme is a summary of the attorney's case, its *raison d'etre.* It should be able to be expressed in a few words or less."[23]

Attorney and legal professor John Shea stated:

> A trial theme is a key component of the lawyer's version of what happened, why it happened, and why the jury is assembled. The theme of the story appeals to the emotions and common sense of the jury about why it happened and who is responsible. For example, the lawyer for the plaintiff in an automobile accident case may tell the jury how the brakes of the car the plaintiff was riding in failed (the "theory"). She may then argue that the case is about much more than just failing brakes; it is a story of an innocent passenger injured by a greedy corporation that failed to take simple measures to insure the safety of its vehicles (the "theme"). The basic themes of this story are "Good versus Evil" and "profits over safety."[24]

Shea cited examples of opposing themes familiar to most jurors that can be incorporated into a trial:

- Good versus evil: e.g., *Cinderella*; *Moby Dick*; Star Wars.
- Man versus nature: e.g., *The Old Man and the Sea*; The Perfect Storm.
- One person against many: e.g., the story of Rosa Parks; the Jackie Robinson story.
- The weak versus the powerful, the underdog defeating the favorite: e.g., Aesop's story of "The Tortoise and the Hare"; the Bible story of David and Goliath; the 1980 U.S. Olympic Hockey Team's "Miracle on Ice."[25]

---

[22] Singer Ph.D., Amy. *Jury-Validated Trial Themes: How to Establish, Enhance, and Employ Such Themes for Courtroom Success.* from http://www.trialconsultants.com/Library/JuryValidatedTrialThemes.html

[23] Ibid.

[24] Shea, John C. *Trial Themes for the Injured Plaintiff.* Marks & Harrison, Richmond, VA. from http://www.marksandharrison.com/pdf/Trial%20Themes.pdf

[25] Shea, John C. *Trial Themes for the Injured Plaintiff.* p. 7.

One of the most memorable trial themes was attorney Johnny Cochran's repeated refrain during his closing arguments at the O.J. Simpson criminal trial in 1995. Cochran repeated a quip he used several times in relation to murder scene gloves that did not fit Simpson's hands: "If it doesn't fit, you must acquit."

Another such theme was used by prosecutors in a court case in Pennsylvania involving Arthur Schirmer, a 64-year-old Methodist minister accused of the 2008 murder of his second wife, Betty Jean Schirmer. Prosecutors dubbed Schirmer the "sinister minister," a theme they repeated throughout the trial. Prosecutors accused Schirmer of murdering both of his wives. In January 2013, a jury in Pennsylvania pronounced him guilty of first-degree murder and evidence tampering in Betty Jean Schirmer's death. He was sentenced in March 2013, the same month he was to go on trial in another Pennsylvania county for the 1999 murder of his first wife, Jewel.

In May 1993, the bodies of three 8-year-old boys, Christopher Byers, Stevie Branch and Michael Moore, were found in a drainage canal in Robin Hood Hills, a wooded area in the poor Arkansas town of West Memphis. Police arrested three men, Damien Echols, Jessie Misskelley Jr., and Jason Baldwin, and charged them with murdering the boys. Juries in two different cases convicted the men in what has come to be known as the 1994 West Memphis Three Murder Trials. Damien Echols was sentenced to death, Jessie Misskelley, Jr. was sentenced to life imprisonment plus two 20-year sentences, and Jason Baldwin was sentenced to life imprisonment. New DNA testing of the evidence resulted in the release of the three suspects in 2011. In his opening statement at the original trial, Prosecutor John Fogleman selected the analogy of a jigsaw puzzle for his theme. Fogleman said:

> Now some lawyers describe the trial of…any kind of law suit, civil, criminal or whatever is [sic] like putting the pieces of a jigsaw puzzle together. Now, any of you who have ever put together a jigsaw puzzle know unless you have the completed picture beside you as you put those pieces together, it's almost impossible to put the pieces together because you don't know what the completed picture looks like. Well, this opening statement is like that completed picture. It gives you a frame of reference, something to look back on as each witness

> testifies or each exhibit comes in as to where that particular piece of evidence fits into the overall picture of the case.[26]

By referring to the jigsaw puzzle theme in his opening statement, Fogleman set up the expectation in the minds of the jurors that all the evidence would formulate a clear picture of the guilt of the accused.

Similarly, each book of the Bible has a compelling theme. Finding that theme is not always easy, but it is critical to understanding any Bible book. In the case of the Gospel of John, finding the theme is simple. John's theme is found in John 20:30-31, the key passage for understanding the Gospel of John:

> Jesus performed many other signs in the presence of his disciples, which are not recorded in this book. But these are written that you may believe that Jesus is the Messiah, the Son of God, and that by believing you may have life in his name.[27]

These verses show that John's goal was to make his case so that people will believe in Jesus. This theme determined everything John communicated in his Gospel.

---

[26] West Memphis Three Trials: The Jesse Misskelley Trial (January 26 - February 4, 1994), Opening Statement of Prosecutor John Fogleman, January 26, 1994, from http://law2.umkc.edu/faculty/projects/ftrials/memphis3/WestMemphis3FoglemanOpening.html

[27] John 20:30-31

3 Opening Statements

Most legal scholars agree that an effective opening statement is vital to the trial process. Studies have shown that 80 percent of jurors' ultimate conclusions with respect to the verdict corresponded with their tentative opinions after opening statements.[28]

> Ladies and gentlemen of the jury, April 19th, 1995, was a beautiful day in Oklahoma City…at least it started out as a beautiful day...
>
> -Joseph Hartzer, Prosecutor,
> *United States of America v. Timothy McVeigh*

In 1995, Attorney General Janet Reno selected Prosecutor Joseph Hartzler to serve as the lead prosecutor in the federal case against Timothy McVeigh for the 1995 bombing of the Alfred P. Murrah Federal Building, an attack that killed 168 people.

> Ladies and gentlemen of the jury, April 19th, 1995, was a beautiful day in Oklahoma City -- at least it started out as a beautiful day. The sun was shining. Flowers were blooming. It was springtime in Oklahoma City. Sometime after six o'clock that morning, Tevin Garrett's mother woke him up to get him ready for the day. He was only 16 months old. He was a toddler; and as some of you know that have experience with toddlers, he had a keen eye for mischief. He would often pull on the cord of her curling iron in the morning, pull it off the counter top until it fell down, often till it fell down on him. That morning, she picked him up and wrestled with him on

[28]http://legal-dictionary.thefreedictionary.com/opening+statement

> her bed before she got him dressed. She remembers this morning because that was the last morning of his life...[29]

In his opening statement, Prosecutor Hartzler personalized the bombing of the Murrah Building by incorporating the names of ordinary people whose lives were forever changed as a result. Hartzler reminded the jury of the terror and the heartbreak stemming from the bombing. In the end, the jury convicted McVeigh on eleven counts of murder and conspiracy. He was executed in 2001.

> On a June evening, the 12th of June, 1994, Nicole Brown Simpson just finished putting her ten-year-old daughter, Sydney, and her six-year-old son, Justin, down to bed. She filled her bathtub with water. She lit some candles, began to get ready to take a bath and relax for the evening. The phone rang. It was 9:40 p.m.[30]

So began the opening arguments presented by Prosecutor Daniel Petrocelli in the 1997 wrongful death civil suit against O.J. Simpson. Simpson was accused of killing Nicole Brown Simpson and Ronald Goldman.

> Nicole answered. And it was her mother, saying that she had left her glasses at the restaurant nearby in Brentwood, where the family had all celebrated Sydney's dance recital over dinner, just an hour before. Nicole's mother asked if Nicole could please pick up her glasses from the restaurant the next day. Nicole said, of course, good-bye, and hung up. Nicole then called the restaurant and asked to speak to a friendly young waiter there. Nicole asked this young waiter if he would be kind enough to drop her mother's glasses off. The young man obliged and said he would drop the glasses off shortly after work, on his way to meet his friend in Marina Del Rey. The young man's name was Ron Goldman. He was 25 years old. He might have run from danger, but he did not. Ron Goldman died, ladies and gentlemen, with his eyes open. And in the last furious moment of his life, Ron saw through

---

[29]http://law2.umkc.edu/faculty/projects/ftrials/mcveigh/prosecutionopen.html. United States of America, Plaintiff, vs. Timothy James McVeigh and Terry Lynn Nichols, Defendants.

[30]http://www.uchastings.edu/academics/faculty/adjunct/sotorosen/classwebsite/docs/Rosen-Great-OpeningStatements-Fall2011.pdf.

> those open eyes the person who killed his friend Nicole. And for that reason, he too had to die. And the last person Ron Goldman saw through his open eyes was the man who took his young life away: The man who now sits in this courtroom, the defendant, Orenthal James Simpson. Ladies and gentlemen, we will prove to you that Ronald Lyle Goldman and Nicole Brown Simpson died at the hands of the defendant, Orenthal Simpson.

Attorneys' opening statements are designed to let the jury know what evidence they will present and what this evidence is supposed to prove. The opening statement is the primary opportunity for attorneys to present their positions to the jury prior to the introduction of the evidence upon which jurors will base their decisions. Opening statements advance frameworks that reveal how attorneys want jurors to view a case. This is an important component since jurors will process evidence in light of whichever framework they adopt.

In 1934, the Supreme Court characterized an opening statement as "ordinarily intended to do no more than to inform the jury in a general way of the nature of the action and defense so that they may better be prepared to understand the evidence."[31]

John's Opening Statement

John began his Gospel with an opening statement that, like an opening statement in a court trial, revealed to the jury (John's readers) what he expected the evidence to prove.

> In the beginning was the Word,
> and the Word was with God,
> and the Word was God.[32]

John's opening line made reference to Genesis 1:1 and rang with power and authority as John announced to the world that, when Jesus arrived on earth, God had come. Once John had everyone's attention with the opening verse, he continued...

[31] Best v. District of Columbia, 291 U.S. 411, 54 S. Ct. 487, 78 L. Ed. 882 (1934)
[32] John 1:1

> He was with God in the beginning. Through him all things were made; without him nothing was made that has been made. In him was life, and that life was the light of all mankind. The light shines in the darkness, and the darkness has not overcome it. There was a man sent from God whose name was John. He came as a witness to testify concerning that light, so that through him all might believe. He himself was not the light; he came only as a witness to the light. The true light that gives light to everyone was coming into the world. He was in the world, and though the world was made through him, the world did not recognize him. He came to that which was his own, but his own did not receive him. Yet to all who did receive him, to those who believed in his name, he gave the right to become children of God— children born not of natural descent, nor of human decision or a husband's will, but born of God. The Word became flesh and made his dwelling among us. We have seen his glory, the glory of the one and only Son, who came from the Father, full of grace and truth. (John testified concerning him. He cried out, saying, "This is the one I spoke about when I said, 'He who comes after me has surpassed me because he was before me.'") Out of his fullness we have all received grace in place of grace already given. For the law was given through Moses; grace and truth came through Jesus Christ. No one has ever seen God, but the one and only Son, who is himself God and is in closest relationship with the Father, has made him known.[33]

In John's opening statement, known to theologians as the prologue, John laid out what he expected his Gospel to show—that Jesus is God who came to earth to give us life. John made three sweeping announcements in this opening statement:

First, John expected the evidence to show that *Jesus is and has always been everything that God is; that Jesus, being God, is creator of the universe; and that Jesus is humanity's only hope for rescue from this dark world.* Second, John expected the evidence to show that, *although many people did not recognize Jesus for who he was, others did recognize him and testified to his divine nature.* Many people alive at the time Jesus lived should have known who Jesus was, but they failed to recognize him. Jewish religious leaders and members of Jesus' own family were in this group. But there were others who indeed did come to

[33] John 1:2-18

recognize Jesus for who he really was. Among those who recognized Jesus was the wild-eyed, itinerant preacher, John the Baptizer.

Finally, John expected the evidence to show that, *as God, Jesus came into our world, became a human being, revealed his identity, and offers eternal life to everyone who will receive him.* Verses 14 and 18 tell us that this divine Jesus took on skin to live among humanity and to reveal his true identity.

> The Word became flesh and made his dwelling among us. We have seen his glory, the glory of the one and only Son, who came from the Father, full of grace and truth.[34]

> No one has ever seen God, but the one and only Son, who is himself God and is in closest relationship with the Father, has made him known.[35]

In verses 12-13 and 17, John wrote that Jesus offers eternal life to everyone who will receive him.

> Yet to all who did receive him, to those who believed in his name, he gave the right to become children of God—children born not of natural descent, nor of human decision or a husband's will, but born of God…For the law was given through Moses; grace and truth came through Jesus Christ.[36]

In accordance with John's theme stated in John 20:30-31, John will use all of his legal strategies for the purpose of convincing people to believe that Jesus is the Christ, and that through believing, those who receive Christ would have eternal life. This means that every reader of John's Gospel simultaneously becomes a member of the jury with the grave responsibility of rendering a verdict on who Jesus is.

The Prosecution's Opening Statement

The prosecution's opening statement will be delivered by the lead prosecutor, Mr. Shaytan Diablo Kakos.

> Ladies and gentlemen of the jury…

---

[34] John 1:14
[35] John 1:18
[36] John 1:12-13, 17

(Shaytan Kakos points to Jesus)

Does this man look like a god to you?

Do not the Scriptures say that "no man has seen God at any time"? And if it is impossible to see God at any time, does not the fact that we can see this man seated at the defense table rule out any possibility that he is God?

Ladies and gentlemen, allow me to introduce myself. My name is Shaytan Diablo Kakos. I will be leading the prosecution in the case against Jesus of Nazareth. Assisting me will be my close colleagues, Miss Paula Ponera and Mr. Ray Skotia. The fact that you are hearing or, as the case may be, reading this opening statement means that you have been placed on the jury for this case. You had no choice but to be on this jury, just as none of us really had any choice as to whether to make a decision concerning this man.

Let me say at the outset that this trial is not a debate about the existence of God. I certainly will not come before you claiming that there is no God. For the Scriptures tell us that it is the fool who has said in his heart, "There is no god." We all come into this chamber believing in God. My team and I certainly believe in God and such belief makes us tremble…

…in reverence, of course!

No, we are not here to argue the existence of God. Rather, the purpose of this trial is to argue whether this man, Jesus of Nazareth, *is* God! You see, this man thinks he is God! Can you believe it? He claims that he himself is the Messiah, the Savior of the world…God! But just look at him! Do you really think that this man, this common looking man…

…is God?

That is what you will have to decide in this case. For we are here to decide if the defendant, Jesus who some call the Christ, is in actuality who he claims he is: the Messiah, the Savior of the world…God! We, of course, do not believe that he is any of those things. The fact that he believes himself to be God does not indeed make him God. Let's face it, how many delusional people do you and I know who think they are God? The evidence will show that this man Jesus is not the Messiah (far from it!), not the Savior of anyone (not even himself!), and certainly not God! The evidence will show that he is nothing more than an ordinary man.

Being on the jury requires that you hear the evidence and render a decision without bias. Your verdict in this trial will affect not only the defendant in the case, but it will also impact you yourselves. For to believe that Jesus is Messiah, Savior, and God is to smack at the worst kind of idolatry, the kind at which even Moses and Abraham would wince! How could the one true and living God wink at such a tragic misbelief? He will not because he cannot!

At the conclusion of this case, you will decide either for or against Jesus the so-called Christ. If you find the evidence to be compelling enough to decide against Jesus the Christ, then you must render a verdict that is against Jesus. I have every reason to believe that, upon hearing and considering the evidence, you will find nothing in this mere man that makes him worthy of your belief and trust.

Now the attorney representing Jesus of Nazareth is a man named John. John is an affable man. You will like him. But that he is a likable man does not mean that he is a believable one.

John will call witnesses; he will present what he calls physical evidence; he will enter into the record so-called prophecies that supposedly foretell Jesus (although they do not!); why, John will even purport to call God to testify, as if that were even possible; all in the name of defending his client. He will do all of these things because, my friends…

...he is desperate!

John wants to convince you that Jesus is the long-promised Messiah. But he has an uphill battle because Jesus' own followers and even his family members ended up forsaking him. For these and many other reasons that will be revealed in this case, Miss Ponera, Mr. Skotia, and I are confident that you will find the arguments of the defense to be insufficient and without the slightest fragment of merit.

You see, ladies and gentlemen, we are here to determine the truth. And truth is that Jesus is not God. He is not the Christ. He is not the Savior of the world. In fact, he could not even save himself, let alone anyone else. Rather, he is nothing more than you or I, an ordinary human being. Therefore, in the interest of truth, I ask you at the conclusion of this trial to decide against Jesus the so-called Christ. Let us put this matter to rest, once and for all. Thank you very much.

4 Calling Witnesses to Testify

It goes without saying that, in courtroom trials, lawyers call witnesses to testify. These witnesses, if credible and consistent in their testimonies, are essential for proving a case.

When Abraham Lincoln was a young attorney practicing law in New Salem, Illinois, a local bully, Jack Armstrong, challenged him to a wrestling match. Lincoln won the match, earning Armstrong's respect and lifelong friendship. Two decades later, in 1857, Lincoln learned that Jack's son William, nicknamed Duff, had been charged with murder. Lincoln's friend Jack had died the year before. Jack Armstong's widow, Hannah, traveled to Springfield and pleaded with Lincoln to save her son from a murder conviction. Lincoln agreed to do so but would accept no fee for his efforts.

The purported facts of the case were these: On the night of August 29, 1857, James Norris and Duff Armstrong engaged in a scuffle with James Metzger during a religious camp meeting near Virgin's Grove, Illinois. These men and many of the witnesses had been drinking heavily. Armstrong allegedly struck Metzger with a slung-shot, a ball made of a lead weight sewn into a leather strap. Metzger left the area where the attack occurred and headed home on his horse, from which he fell a few times on the way. When a doctor examined him the next day, he found that Metzger's skull was fractured in two places. Two days later, Metzger died as a result of his injuries. The sheriff arrested Norris and Armstrong, and a grand jury indicted them for the murder of Metzger. Norris' trial came first. A jury found him guilty of manslaughter and sentenced him to eight years in the state penitentiary. It was then that the widow of Lincoln's friend asked him to take her son's case.

Lincoln filed for a change of venue for Armstrong on grounds that people in Mason county were so prejudiced against Armstrong he would be unable to get a fair trial. The judge granted Lincoln's request, and the case was transferred to the Cass County Courthouse, in Beardstown.

The prosecution's case rested on the testimony of key witness Charles Allen, who claimed he had seen Duff Armstrong murder James Metzger. Allen testified that on August 29, 1857, at approximately 11:00 p.m., at the camp meeting, he saw Duff Armstrong kill James Preston Metzger, using a slung-shot. Despite being at least 150 feet away from the fatal fight, Allen claimed he had a perfect view of the incident thanks to the light of a full moon.

Lincoln had Allen repeat his statement about the brightness of the moon several times. Then Lincoln asked the judge for permission to enter an 1857 almanac into evidence, an extraordinary move at that time, given that the judicial system relied almost solely on witness testimonies. Lincoln asked Allen to read the almanac entry for August 29, 1857. It read "moon rides low," meaning there was no full moon that night, and what moon there was barely rose above the horizon. Based on this excerpt, Lincoln argued that it would have been impossible for Allen to see anything from a distance of 150 feet. Lincoln had successfully discredited the witness. Armstrong's trial was over by the end of the day. After only one ballot, the jury found Armstrong not guilty.[37] The "Almanac Trial," as it came to be known, is probably the most famous court case of Abraham Lincoln's career, immortalized by Henry Fonda in his 1939 film *Young Mr. Lincoln.*

Throughout his Gospel, John called witnesses to testify. Once on the stand, it is as if John asked each witness the same question: "Who do you say that Jesus Christ is?" Below are the witnesses the writer called, and the answers they gave to his questions. Throughout this book, the scriptural verses in italics indicate what the testimony of the person would include.

John's first witness was John the Baptizer. (John 1:6-8, 15, 19-27, 29-36)

John 1:6-8 states that John (the Baptizer) came as a "witness to testify." This not only clued readers in to the testimony of the Baptizer, but also to the forthcoming testimonies of other people in John's Gospel. John would present witnesses who will testify on behalf of Jesus.

[37] From http://rhapsodyinbooks.wordpress.com/2009/05/08/may-8-1858-lincoln%E2%80%99s-most-famous-court-case-the-almanac-trial/ *May 8, 1858: Lincoln's Most Famous Court Case: The Almanac Trial.*

> There was a man sent from God whose name was John. *He came as a witness to testify* concerning that light, so that through him all might believe. He himself was not the light; he came only as a witness to the light.[38]

In the excerpts below from John 1, the italicized portions provide what would be the Baptizer's testimony in the case for Jesus. The picture imagines the prosecuting attorney cross-examining John the Baptizer concerning Jesus.

> (John testified concerning him. He cried out, saying, "*This is the one I spoke about when I said, 'He who comes after me has surpassed me because he was before me.'*")
>
> Now this was John's testimony when the Jewish leaders in Jerusalem sent priests and Levites to ask him who he was. He did not fail to confess, but confessed freely, "*I am not the Messiah.*"
>
> They asked him, "Then who are you? Are you Elijah?"
>
> He said, "*I am not.*"
>
> "Are you the Prophet?"
>
> He answered, "*No.*"
>
> Finally they said, "Who are you? Give us an answer to take back to those who sent us. What do you say about yourself?"
>
> John replied in the words of Isaiah the prophet, "*I am the voice of one calling in the wilderness, 'Make straight the way for the Lord.'*"
>
> Now the Pharisees who had been sent, questioned him, "Why then do you baptize if you are not the Messiah, nor Elijah, nor the Prophet?"
>
> "*I baptize with water,*" John replied, "*but among you stands one you do not know. He is the one who comes after me, the straps of whose sandals I am not worthy to untie.*"[39]

The following verses from John 1 imagine the answers of John the Baptizer to the question of John the attorney: "John, who do you say that Jesus is?"

> The next day John saw Jesus coming toward him and said, "*Look, the Lamb of God, who takes away the sin of*

[38] John 1:6-8

[39] John 1:15, 19-27

> *the world! This is the one I meant when I said, 'A man who comes after me has surpassed me because he was before me.' I myself did not know him, but the reason I came baptizing with water was that he might be revealed to Israel.*"
>
> Then John gave this testimony: "*I saw the Spirit come down from heaven as a dove and remain on him. And I myself did not know him, but the one who sent me to baptize with water told me, 'The man on whom you see the Spirit come down and remain is the one who will baptize with the Holy Spirit.' I have seen and I testify that this is God's Chosen One.*" The next day John was there again with two of his disciples. When he saw Jesus passing by, he said, "*Look, the Lamb of God!*"[40]

The testimony of John the Baptizer might read like this:

Prosecutor Shaytan Kakos:	Will you please state your name for the court?
John the Baptizer:	John. Some call me the Baptizer.
Prosecutor Shaytan Kakos:	Why do people call you the Baptizer?
John the Baptizer:	I guess it is because I have baptized a lot of people.
	(Scattered laughter in the courtroom)
Prosecutor Shaytan Kakos:	Very well, Mr. John the Baptizer, since you baptize a lot of people, are you then the Messiah?
John the Baptizer:	Oh, goodness no! I am not the Messiah. Far from it!
Prosecutor Shaytan Kakos:	Then who are you? Are you Elijah?
John the Baptizer:	No, I am not Elijah.
Prosecutor Shaytan Kakos:	Are you the Prophet?
John the Baptizer:	No, I am not the Prophet.
Prosecutor Shaytan Kakos:	Who are you then? Give us an answer. What do you have to say about yourself?
John the Baptizer:	I am just an itinerant preacher, like a voice calling in the wilderness, "Make straight the way for the Lord."

[40] John 1:29-36

Prosecutor Shaytan Kakos:	A voice? What on earth does that mean? If you are not the Messiah, nor Elijah, nor the Prophet, then why do you baptize people?
John the Baptizer:	I merely baptize with water, but right here in this court-room is someone you do not recognize. You should, but you don't. His ministry has come after mine, but he is much more than I will ever be. I am not worthy to untie the straps of his sandals. I baptize people to get them ready for him!
Prosecutor Shaytan Kakos:	In reality, your baptism means absolutely nothing, is that not correct, Mr. John Baptizer? No further questions, your Honor.
Judge:	Defense's witness.
John:	John, do you know Jesus?
John the Baptizer:	I do. We are family.
John:	How are you related to Jesus?
John the Baptizer:	We are cousins.
John:	You are the one who baptized Jesus. Are you not?
John the Baptizer:	Yes, I did baptize Jesus. I baptized him in the Jordan River.
John:	Something special occurred when Jesus was baptized, did it not?
John the Baptizer:	Oh, yes indeed!
John:	Tell us what happened.
John the Baptizer:	When I baptized him, I witnessed the Spirit of God come down from heaven as a dove and rest upon him.
John:	Would it be correct to say that you have baptized quite a few people in your ministry, John?

John the Baptizer: Well, I do not know the exact number, but yes, I have baptized a lot of people over the years.

John: Have you ever seen the Spirit of God descend upon a person being baptized like the Spirit did when you were baptizing Jesus?

John the Baptizer: Never! I have never seen that happen at any other time other than when I baptized Jesus.

John: I would guess that experience made quite an impression on you.

John the Baptizer: Oh, I'll say it did!

John: So tell us, John. What is your opinion of Jesus?

John the Baptizer: I cannot say enough good about him. He is the one I was talking about when I said, "He who comes after me has surpassed me because he has always been before me."

John: John, I am sure you are aware that there are people who would like nothing better than to discredit Jesus, people who will do everything in their power to bring him down. They will say he is demon-possessed, an imposter, a fraud, just another charlatan. So, tell us. Who do you believe Jesus is?

John the Baptizer: I believe Jesus is the Lamb of God who forgives the sin of everyone who will believe in him! This is the man I was talking about when I said, "A man who comes after me has surpassed me because he was before me." At first, even I did not fully realize who he was, but I came to realize that the reason God called me to baptize people with water was so that

Jesus might be revealed to Israel as well as to the whole world.

John: John, what would you say to those people who do not know Jesus the way you have come to know him and, therefore, insist on condemning him?

John the Baptizer: I say again that I myself did not fully know him, but the one who sent me to baptize with water told me, "The man on whom you see the Spirit come down and remain is the one who will baptize with the Holy Spirit." Well, that's exactly what I saw happen, and I'm telling you, there's no question about it so far as I am concerned: This man is the Son of God.

John: No further questions. Thank you.

Prosecutor Shaytan Kakos: Your Honor, if it pleases the court, the prosecution has a few more questions for this witness.

Judge: Very well.

Prosecutor Shaytan Kakos: Is it true, Mr. John Baptizer, that while in prison in Machaerus, you came to doubt whether Jesus was the Savior?

John the Baptizer: Yes, that is true, but—

Prosecutor Shaytan Kakos: And is it not also true that, not only did you come to doubt whether Jesus was the Savior, but you no longer considered him to be the Messiah, and started looking for someone else to be the long promised Messiah?

John the Baptizer: Well, I—

Prosecutor Shaytan Kakos: A simple 'yes' or 'no' will suffice, Sir!

John the Baptizer: Yes.

Prosecutor Shaytan Kakos: One more question, Mr. Baptizer. If Jesus of Nazareth had really been Messiah and God, then he could have

	easily rescued you from prison and spared your life from being beheaded, is that not true?
John the Baptizer:	I did not expect—
Prosecutor Shaytan Kakos:	Once again, sir, a simple 'yes' or 'no' is all that is called for!
John the Baptizer:	Yes, it is true.
Prosecutor Shaytan Kakos:	Thank you, sir. No further questions, your Honor.

The second witness was Andrew, Simon Peter's brother. (John 1:40-42) In Andrew's testimony, one can imagine the attorney asking the question, "Andrew, after you met Jesus Christ, can you tell us what you told your brother about him?" The italicized portion of verses 40-42 gives Andrew's answer.

> Andrew, Simon Peter's brother, was one of the two who heard what John had said and who had followed Jesus. The first thing Andrew did was to find his brother Simon and tell him, "*We have found the Messiah*" (that is, the Christ). And he brought him to Jesus.[41]

The brief testimony of Andrew might read like this:

John:	Andrew, after you met Jesus, you immediately ran to your brother, Simon. Is that right?
Andrew:	Yes, that is right.
John:	And what did you tell Simon when you located him?
Andrew:	I told him we had found the Messiah.
John:	And by "Messiah," whom were you talking about?
Andrew:	I was referring to Jesus.
John:	So is it true that you believe that Jesus is the Messiah who was prophesied in the Old Testament?

[41] John 1:40-42.

Andrew:	Absolutely! I do!
John:	Thank you, Andrew. No further questions, your Honor.
Judge:	Prosecution's witness.
Prosecutor Shaytan Kakos:	Mr. Andrew, do you remember the day Jesus was executed?
Andrew:	Yes, I certainly do.
Prosecutor Shaytan Kakos:	Can you describe in detail for the court what happened at Jesus' interrogation and crucifixion?
Andrew:	Well, I—
Prosecutor Shaytan Kakos:	What is the matter, Mr. Andrew? Being a close follower of Jesus, surely you were present at the execution of Jesus, were you not?
Andrew:	Uh, no, sir, I was not there.
Prosecutor Shaytan Kakos:	Oh, I am sorry! It was not my intention to embarrass you, Mr. Andrew! I would not have asked you that question had I known that you did not even bother to show up for Jesus at his execution. I just assumed that since you were one of Jesus' closest followers, you would certainly have been present at his execution. Please forgive me! No more questions for this witness, your Honor!

The third witness was Philip. (John 1:44-45)

John 1:44-45 tells us about a young man named Philip, who, upon meeting Jesus, ran to his friend Nathanael to tell him about Jesus. The italicized portion indicates Philip's testimony.

> Philip, like Andrew and Peter, was from the town of Bethsaida. Philip found Nathanael and told him, "*We have found the one Moses wrote about in the Law, and about whom the prophets also wrote—Jesus of Nazareth, the son of Joseph.*"[42]

---

[42] John 1:44-45.

Philip's testimony might resemble the following conversation:

John:	Please state your name for the court.
Philip:	My name is Philip.
John:	Philip, you have met Jesus, correct?
Philip:	Yes, I have.
John:	And are you a follower of Jesus?
Philip:	Yes, I have followed him now for a little over three years.
John:	When you first met Jesus, is it true that you immediately told people about your encounter with him?
Philip:	I did. I went to my friend Nathanael and told him about Jesus.
John:	And what did you say to Nathanael about Jesus?
Philip:	I told him that we had found the one whom Moses wrote about in the Law, and about whom the prophets also wrote, Jesus of Nazareth, the son of Joseph, the Messiah.
John:	So, you believe Jesus is the Messiah?
Philip:	Without a doubt, I believe that Jesus is the Messiah. Yes.
Judge:	Does the prosecution wish to question the witness?
Prosecutor Shaytan Kakos:	We have no questions for this witness, your Honor.

The fourth witness was Nathanael. (John 1:44-49)

When Philip told Nathanael about Jesus being the Messiah from Nazareth, Nathanael was skeptical. "Nazareth!" he said, "Can anything good come from there?"[43] Philip invited Nathanael to come see for himself. As the two of them approached Jesus, Jesus said something that indicated he knew about Nathanael even though the two of them had not officially met. The

[43] John 1:46

italicized words in Nathanael's response below indicate what his testimony would be.

> When Jesus saw Nathanael approaching, he said of him, "Here is a true Israelite, in whom there is nothing false."
> "How do you know me?" Nathanael asked.
> Jesus answered, "I saw you while you were still under the fig tree, before Philip called you."
> Then Nathanael declared, "*Rabbi, you are the Son of God; you are the King of Israel.*"[44]

Nathanael's courtroom testimony might sound like this:

John:	Nathanael, you have met Jesus who is called Christ, correct?
Nathanael:	Yes, I have.
John:	Is it correct that, at first, you were skeptical about Jesus being who your friend Philip said he was?
Nathanael:	Yes, I would have to say that I do not care much for the people of Nazareth. I could hardly believe that anything or anyone good could come from there.
John:	When you finally met Jesus, something surprising happened. Can you please tell the court what you found that was so surprising?
Nathanael:	He acted as though he knew me. He described me to the hilt even though we had never met.
John:	So what do you think of Jesus now?
Nathanael:	I believe he is the Son of God; he is the King of Israel.
John:	I'm assuming your meeting with Jesus has changed the way you view people from Nazareth. Is that a safe assumption, Nathanael?

[44] John 1:47-49

Nathanael:	Yes, it has.
John:	Thank you, Nathanael. No further questions. You may step down.
Judge:	Prosecution's witness.
Prosecutor Shaytan Kakos:	Nathanael, please tell me, have you and I ever met or had a conversation with each other?
Nathanael:	No, I do not believe we have.
Prosecutor Shaytan Kakos:	Do you think it is possible for me to know at least something about you even though I have never met you before today?
Nathanael:	Yes, of course!
Prosecutor Shaytan Kakos:	So, the fact that Jesus knew something about you before he even officially met you is not all that unique, is it?
Nathanael:	Oh! I—I guess not!
Prosecutor Shaytan Kakos:	Of course not! No further questions, your Honor.

The next witnesses were a mixed-race Samaritan woman Jesus met at a well and her neighbors and family. (John 4)

The writer of the Gospel of John highlighted the testimonies of women, a gesture unheard of in first century culture where women were not allowed to testify in court and were rarely included in documents such as family trees (cf. Luke's genealogy of Jesus in Luke 3). In John 4, the writer highlighted not only a woman, but a broken woman from a half-breed race.

> Now Jesus learned that the Pharisees had heard that he was gaining and baptizing more disciples than John— although in fact it was not Jesus who baptized, but his disciples. So he left Judea and went back once more to Galilee.
>
> Now he had to go through Samaria. So he came to a town in Samaria called Sychar, near the plot of ground Jacob had given to his son Joseph. Jacob's well was there, and Jesus, tired as he was from the journey, sat down by the well. It was about noon. When a Samaritan woman came to draw water, Jesus said to her, "Will you give me a drink?" (His disciples had gone into the town to buy food.)

> The Samaritan woman said to him, "You are a Jew and I am a Samaritan woman. How can you ask me for a drink?" (For Jews do not associate with Samaritans.)
>
> Jesus answered her, "If you knew the gift of God and who it is that asks you for a drink, you would have asked him and he would have given you living water."[45]

Sensing rising opposition from the Pharisees in Judea, Jesus and his disciples traveled from Jerusalem in the south to Galilee in the north. When traveling from Jerusalem to Galilee, most devout Jews took the long route, crossing the Jordan River eastward into Jordan, moving northward past Samaria, then crossing westward back over the Jordan River into Galilee. They did this to avoid going through the region of Samaria because most Jews hated the Samaritans who lived there. The Samaritans originated from people who lived in what had been the Northern Kingdom of Israel. When Assyria invaded the Northern Kingdom in 722 B.C.E. and carried its people into captivity, the king of Assyria sent people from other parts of Assyria to inhabit Samaria (2 Kings 17:24; Ezra 4:2-11). These foreigners intermarried with the Israelite population that remained in Samaria. The resulting offspring were called Samaritans. Although they worshiped God as did the Jews, their religion was not mainstream Judaism. They accepted only the first five books of the Bible, and their temple was on Mount Gerazim instead of on Mount Zion in Jerusalem.

John noted that Jesus felt compelled to go to Samaria. But rather than travel the traditional long route, Jesus took his disciples along the quickest route which ran straight through Samaria. Reaching Jacob's Well, Jesus sent his disciples to a market for food in the nearby village of Sychar while he rested at the well. John noted that it was about noon, the hottest part of the day, when a Samaritan woman came to the well to draw water. She came to draw water at that time of the day, instead of the usual morning or evening times, so she wouldn't be seen by others. People shunned the woman because of her failed marital relationships. As one writer put it, this woman was marginalized.

> When you are marginalized, you have a whole different set of rules that you live by. You know where you can go and where you can't. You know who you can talk to and who you can't...

---

[45] John 4:1-10

> who accepts you and who does not. And something else happens to you when you are marginalized...something internal. You begin to think of yourself as less than, and in some cases even deserving of the poor treatment you receive...To be marginalized means to see yourself as different...separate from...broken...not normal.[46]

Country music artist Miranda Lambert has a song, "Famous in a Small Town," that aptly describes this woman's predicament.

> Every grandma, in-law, ex-girlfriend
> Maybe knows you just a little too well
> Whether you're late for church or you're stuck in jail
> Hey word's gonna get around
> Everybody dies famous in a small town.[47]

Certainly this woman's past had made her famous in her village. The writer meant for us to see that this woman came alone.[48] Karoline Lewis observes that John made this woman's plight more noticeable by placing her story immediately after the story of Nicodemus in John 3.[49] The contrast between Nicodemus and the Samaritan woman is striking. Nicodemus was a Pharisee, a man with a notable name, a great reputation, and a leader of the Jews. He came to Jesus under the cover of night. The woman, on the other hand, was a Samaritan, a religious and political outsider; she was an outcast with no name, but she met Jesus in full daylight.

By reaching out to the woman, Jesus violated three Jewish customs: first, Jesus spoke to a woman in public, which was discouraged; second, he spoke to a Samaritan woman, which, in Jewish minds, was worse; and third, he requested that she get him a drink of water from Jacob's Well, which would have made Jesus ceremonially unclean according to Jewish law.[50]

---

[46] http://www.theologicalstew.com/water-woman-at-the-well.html
[47] Writer(s): Miranda Leigh Lambert, Miranda Lambert, Travis Howard. Copyright: Watsky Music LLC, Sony/ATV Tree Publishing, Nashville Star Music, Watsky Music.
[48] http://revgalblogpals.org/2014/01/27/narrative-lectionary-in-laws-outlaws-ex-girlfriends-john-41-42/
[49] Commentary on John 4:5-42 by Karoline Lewis. From http://www.workingpreacher.org/preaching.aspx?commentary_id=44
[50] Woman at the Well - Bible Story Summary: Jesus Shocks the Woman at the Well With His Love and Acceptance, by Jack Zavada. http://christianity.about.com/od/biblestorysummaries/a/Woman-At-The-Well.htm

Jesus told the woman he could give her "living water" so that she would never thirst again. Jesus used the words "living water" to refer to eternal life. At first, the Samaritan woman did not fully understand Jesus' meaning. Then, although Jesus and the woman had never met before, Jesus revealed that he knew she had been married to five husbands and that she was now living with a man who was not her husband. At that point, the woman realized that Jesus was no ordinary man, and she was embarrassed that Jesus knew such intimate details of her life. So she tried to change the subject.

> "Sir," the woman said, "I can see that you are a prophet. Our ancestors worshiped on this mountain, but you Jews claim that the place where we must worship is in Jerusalem."
>
> "Woman," Jesus replied, "believe me, a time is coming when you will worship the Father neither on this mountain nor in Jerusalem. You Samaritans worship what you do not know; we worship what we do know, for salvation is from the Jews. Yet a time is coming and has now come when the true worshipers will worship the Father in the Spirit and in truth, for they are the kind of worshipers the Father seeks. God is spirit, and his worshipers must worship in the Spirit and in truth."
>
> The woman said, "I know that Messiah" (called Christ) "is coming. When he comes, he will explain everything to us."
>
> Then Jesus declared, "I, the one speaking to you—I am he."[51]

By the time the disciples returned from their grocery shopping, the woman had left Jesus at the well and returned home to her family, telling them she had seen the Christ. Her words form what would be her testimony in trial.

> Then, leaving her water jar, the woman went back to the town and said to the people, "*Come, see a man who told me everything I ever did. Could this be the Christ?*"[52]

---

[51] John 4:19-26
[52] John 4:28-29

The transcripts of her testimony might look like this:

John:	Lady, you met Jesus at Jacob's Well one day at noon. Is this correct?
The Woman:	Yes, that is true, but I did not plan to meet him. He was already there when I arrived. I did nothing wrong; he was perched at the well when I got there, I assure you, and—
John:	Ma'am, you are not on trial here. You have nothing to worry about. Just relax and answer my questions.
The Woman:	Well, that's what I'm trying to do! But I just want everybody to know that I—
John:	Just relax. You have nothing to worry about. We only have a few simple questions. That is all.
The Woman:	Well, all right. I just, well, okay.
John:	Could you tell us what happened on the day you met Jesus at the well?
The Woman:	Well, I usually go to the well alone, at noon, to draw water for my family. I am not used to anyone being there at that time. But, that day, when I arrived at the well, this man was perched on the other side of the well.
John:	And this man was Jesus?
The Woman:	Yes, it was Jesus. But I want you all to know that I had no idea anyone would be there!
John:	We understand. You expected to be at the well alone.
The Woman:	That is right.
John:	Okay. What happened next?
The Woman:	He, Jesus, asked me for some water. His request took me by surprise because people do not normally talk to

me; plus, it is inappropriate for a woman, especially a Samaritan woman like me, to have a conversation with a man, let alone a Jewish man. I inquired of him why he asked me for water. He said he could offer me a special kind of water—living water, he called it—and that if I drank this water, I would never thirst again.

John: Did you ask Jesus for some of this special water?

The Woman: Yes, I did.

John: And then what happened?

The Woman: Well, he…he told me to go fetch my, my husband.

John: And this was a problem?

The Woman: Yes.

John: Why was this such a problem?

The Woman: Well, it is embarrassing for me. I have been married five times, and, um, the man I am currently living with is not my husband.

John: So your marriage situation is the reason you normally come alone to the well?

The Woman: It is. I just got tired of being talked about. *(The woman looks down.)* I, uh, I got tired of the cutting looks.

John: Had you ever met Jesus before?

The Woman: No, I had not. I had never even seen him before.

John: And yet he knew all about you.

The Woman: Yes, he did! He told me things about me that should have been kept secret. The fact that he knew such things about me took me off-guard. I tried to change the subject.

John:	How do you think he came to know all these things?
The Woman:	That's what I wanted to know! He must have talked to several of the people in town to know all he said about me. But some of the things he said, only I knew!
John:	So, as a result of your conversation with him at the well, what do you think about this man Jesus?
The Woman:	This man knew things about me no one knows. He recited to me everything I have ever done. How could he not be the Christ?
John:	Thank you.
Judge:	Does the Prosecution wish to question the witness?
Prosecutor Shaytan Kakos:	No, your Honor. It is bad enough that we have to call women to testify at all in this case, let alone a woman of such questionable character as this woman. Who could possibly believe her?
John:	Objection, your Honor! This woman is not on trial here!
Prosecutor Shaytan Kakos:	Withdrawn! Besides, I too know things about this woman even though, before today, I had never met her. But that certainly does not make me the Messiah! Knowing about this woman's past does not make Jesus the Messiah either!

Upon leaving the well, the woman returned home and told her family about her encounter with Jesus. As a result, the woman's family came back with her to the well. John did not record most of their conversation with Jesus, but it is clear that the woman's relatives were so impressed with Jesus that they urged him to stay with them for a few days. Jesus stayed with the Samaritans for two days. The italicized words below indicate not only the woman's testimony, but also the testimonies of her townspeople.

> Many of the Samaritans from that town believed in him because of the woman's testimony, "*He told me everything I ever did.*" So when the Samaritans came to him, they urged him to stay with them, and he stayed two days. And because of his words many more became believers. They said to the woman, "We no longer believe just because of what you said; *now we have heard for ourselves, and we know that this man really is the Savior of the world.*"[53]

John:	Sir, you live in a small town in Samaria, is that right?
Samaritan:	Yes, I do.
John:	Are you acquainted with the woman who testified to having talked with Jesus at Jacob's Well?
Samaritan:	Yes, I know her.
John:	When she returned home after her conversation with Jesus, how did she seem? Was she different?
Samaritan:	She was very excited. I had never seen her so animated.
John:	What did she say?
Samaritan:	She said she had met a man named Jesus. She urged us to come meet this man, that he had told her everything she had ever done, even though they had never met.
John:	And did you believe her?
Samaritan:	Well, not right away. We did not *dis*believe her. We just needed to see for ourselves whether what she was saying was true.
John:	So you went with the woman back to the well and met Jesus.
Samaritan:	We did.
John:	And what did you conclude after having met Jesus?

[53] John 4:39-42

Samaritan:	We heard him for ourselves and were amazed! It became clear to us that this man really is the Savior of the world.

John called to the stand people from the crowds who observed Jesus. (John 7)

In John 6, Jesus taught and performed miraculous signs in the presence of large crowds. Predictably, the crowds' reactions were mixed. In chapter 7, John recorded both the unfavorable and the favorable responses of people. He then highlighted the positive testimonies of these people. The following verses reveal the people's responses to Jesus.

> Among the crowds there was widespread whispering about him. Some said, "*He is a good man.*"
>
> Not until halfway through the festival did Jesus go up to the temple courts and begin to teach. The Jews there were amazed and asked, "*How did this man get such learning without having been taught?*"
>
> Still, many in the crowd believed in him. They said, "*When the Messiah comes, will he perform more signs than this man?*"
>
> On hearing his words, some of the people said, "*Surely this man is the Prophet.*"
>
> Others said, "*He is the Messiah.*"[54]

The dialogue below imagines John questioning one person from among the crowds.

John:	Sir, were you among the crowds who saw Jesus performing miracles and teaching at the festival in Jerusalem?
Man:	I was.
John:	Had you ever met Jesus before, or heard him teach?

[54] John 7:12, 14-15, 31, 40-41

Man: I had heard of him, but I had never met him or heard him in person.

John: Had you formed an opinion of Jesus prior to meeting him?

Man: Never thought much about it. Then again, I've never given much credence to miracle workers.

John: And now that you have heard Jesus teaching, and witnessed him performing miracles, what do you think about him?

Man: Well, I think he is definitely a good man. No doubt about that! The more I heard him, the more I wondered how he amassed such knowledge without having been taught. Then I observed Jesus doing things that are, well, impossible for anyone to do, and I was in awe. My thought was that when the Messiah comes, will he perform more signs than this man? After having seen him for myself, I am convinced that he is the Prophet, the Messiah.

John: Thank you, sir. You may step down.

The next witnesses were the Temple guards sent to arrest Jesus. (John 7)
Among the responses of people recorded by John in chapter 7 are those from the Temple guards. The role of the Temple guards was to ensure that everything in the Temple was in order, that nothing in the Temple was disturbed during the night, and all of the sacred vessels needed to perform the priestly service were accessible and in their proper places. In addition to these responsibilities, the guards followed any other instructions given to them by the religious leaders. These extra responsibilities included locating and arresting Jesus. Enlisting the Temple guards to testify on Jesus' behalf was a stroke of genius on John's part because, although they were not believers in Jesus and therefore could not be charged with bias toward Jesus, their testimonies bolstered John's case for Jesus.

> Finally the temple guards went back to the chief priests and Pharisees, who asked them, "Why didn't you bring him in?"
>
> "*No one ever spoke the way this man does,*" the guards declared.[55]

The guards' testimonies would necessarily be brief. John did not want them saying more than he needed them to say, so he would have to carefully phrase his questions to them. Their testimonies might look like the one below.

John:	Sir, can you tell us your occupation?
Guard:	I am a Temple guard.
John:	What exactly does a Temple guard do?
Guard:	We guard the Temple.
	(Scattered laughter throughout the courtroom.)
John:	But what does it mean to guard the Temple? Do you just stand guard outside the Temple at all times? Exactly what are your duties?
Guard:	We keep a strict watch over the Temple at all times. In particular we make sure that nothing sacrilegious occurs in or around the Temple, no one unclean enters the Temple. Beyond that, we also serve at the discretion of the High Priest and the Pharisees. Anything they instruct us to do, we do it.
John:	What about with regards to Jesus? Did the religious leaders give you any instructions concerning Jesus?
Guard:	They did. The Chief Priests and the Pharisees ordered us to find Jesus and then arrest him.
John:	Why did they want Jesus arrested?
Guard:	You will have to ask them, sir. We simply follow orders.

[55] John 7:45-46

John: Very well. As I understand it, you found Jesus, but did not arrest him. Is that correct, that you did not arrest Jesus?

Guard: Yes, that is correct.

John: So why did you not arrest Jesus?

Guard: Well, at first, Jesus proved to be quite elusive. He just seemed to disappear into the crowds. Every time we looked for him, we could not find him.

John: At some point, though, you were in a position to apprehend Jesus, but you did not. Why did you not arrest Jesus when you did have the opportunity?

Guard: Honestly, several of us who heard him were spellbound by his words. Our superiors asked us why we did not arrest him. But how could we? We never witnessed him breaking any laws and, well, frankly, we had never heard anyone speak the way this man did.

John: Thank you, sir. No further questions.

Judge: Mr. Kakos, your witness.

Asst. Prosecutor Ray Scotia: I will be the one questioning this witness, your Honor.

Judge: Very well, Mr. Skotia. You may proceed with the witness.

Asst. Prosecutor Ray Scotia: Thank you, your Honor. Sir, you said you had never heard anyone speak the way Jesus spoke. Is that correct?

Guard: Yes, sir. That is correct.

Asst. Prosecutor Ray Scotia: Does the fact that someone is a dynamic speaker qualify him or her to be God or the Savior of the world?

Guard: Well, no, I do not suppose so.

Asst. Prosecutor Ray Scotia: No, of course not! Tell me, sir. Historically, when the Chief Priests have had suspicions about some rebel

	rouser, has it been your experience that they have been right to be suspicious about them?
Guard:	I would have to say yes. In my experience, they are almost always right when they are suspicious of someone.
Asst. Prosecutor Ray Scotia:	And do they always communicate the specifics of their suspicions to the Temple guards?
Guard:	No, Sir. They do not.
Asst. Prosecutor Ray Scotia:	So, when they instructed you to arrest Jesus, they probably had some very good reasons for doing so, reasons that they did not convey to you, would you say that would most likely be the truth?
Guard:	Well, I suppose it would.
Asst. Prosecutor Ray Scotia:	That's what I thought. Thank you. No further questions.

John called on some of the Jewish religious leaders to testify, but they refused. (John 12)

John noted that some of the Jewish religious leaders secretly believed in Jesus. John called on the religious leaders who believed in Jesus to testify, but they refused to testify because they feared that other religious leaders might punish them for their testimonies.

> …at the same time many even among the leaders believed in him. But because of the Pharisees they would not confess their faith for fear they would be put out of the synagogue; for they loved praise from men more than praise from God.[56]

John called the rest of the disciples. (John 16)

John 16 finds Jesus trying to prepare his disciples for his departure. As noted above, Jesus promised them the help of the Holy Spirit to overcome the difficulties they would face. Beginning with verse 25, Jesus spoke more clearly

---

[56] John 12:42-43

concerning the fact that he would be leaving and going back to his Father. The disciples responded to Jesus' clearer message with stronger faith.

> "Though I have been speaking figuratively, a time is coming when I will no longer use this kind of language but will tell you plainly about my Father. In that day you will ask in my name. I am not saying that I will ask the Father on your behalf. No, the Father himself loves you because you have loved me and have believed that I came from God. I came from the Father and entered the world; now I am leaving the world and going back to the Father."
>
> Then Jesus' disciples said, "*Now you are speaking clearly and without figures of speech. Now we can see that you know all things and that you do not even need to have anyone ask you questions. This makes us believe that you came from God.*"[57]

Assuming that John called any of Jesus' disciples to the witness stand at this point, John might ask them how they felt about Jesus once Jesus had spoken more clearly to them.

John:	Is it true that you followed Jesus for over three years?
Disciple:	Yes, I did.
John:	During that time, how often would you say you heard Jesus speak, probably, hundreds of times?
Disciple:	Yes, hundreds of times.
John:	How was Jesus as a speaker? Did you understand him? Did he clearly communicate when he spoke?
Disciple:	Jesus was a powerful speaker. People were mesmerized every time he spoke. Thousands of people responded to his teaching. Honestly, though, this was not always the case with me. I often had difficulty understanding what Jesus said. He told a lot of stories, and used many

[57] John 16:25-30

analogies and metaphors, without just coming out and telling us what he meant by them. Now, don't get me wrong; there were always people who understood what he meant by them. But, being a more literal-minded person, I prefer straightforward talk.

John: Was there ever a time when you heard Jesus speaking in a more straightforward, direct manner?

Disciple: Yes, there was. I am not sure exactly what brought about the change, but right at the last, he began speaking in a clearer, more forthright manner.

John: How did you respond when Jesus would speak more clearly?

Disciple: I loved it! It made me realize that he knew all things and that he did not need for anyone to ask him questions. In fact, I told him that I appreciated that he was speaking more clearly.

John: Did Jesus' clearer messages at the end strengthen your belief in him or weaken your faith in him?

Disciple: Oh, strengthened my faith in him! Once I understood what he was saying, I believed without a doubt that he came from God.

John: Thank you! No further questions.

Judge: Prosecution's witness!

Asst. Prosecutor Ray Scotia: So, let me get this straight. At first, you had difficulty understanding Jesus because you say he did not speak so clearly. But then, he started speaking so understandably that, in your words, you believed without a doubt that Jesus came from God. Is that correct?

Disciple:	That is correct. Without a doubt!
Asst. Prosecutor Ray Scotia:	Yet, at the time Jesus was interrogated and then later crucified, you ran away. You were nowhere to be found. At his most trying moment, you were noticeably absent. Now, does that sound like someone who believes, as you said, without a doubt?
Disciple:	Well, I, uh—
Asst. Prosecutor Ray Scotia:	Oh, no need to respond. You already have responded! You responded when you forsook the one you believed in "without a doubt"!

John called other witnesses to testify on behalf of Jesus. We will hear their testimonies at later junctures in this book. At this point in the trial, John examined the faces of the jury. While he could not read all the jurors, it was clear that not all of them were convinced that Jesus was the Christ.

5 Presenting Physical Evidence (Miraculous Signs)

As a child born in France in the 1870s, Edmond Locard immersed himself in the Sherlock Holmes detective mysteries of Arthur Conan Doyle. Locard later trained as a medical examiner under the great French criminal investigator Alphonse Bertillon and became a pioneer in forensic science, opening the world's first crime scene investigation lab in Lyons, France, in 1910. Serving in World War I, Locard identified causes and locations of soldiers' deaths by analyzing stains left on their uniforms. He became known as the "Sherlock Holmes of France." Locard formulated the basic principle of forensic science: "Every contact leaves a trace." This became known as Locard's exchange principle. Locard said, "It is impossible for a criminal to act, especially considering the intensity of a crime, without leaving traces of his presence."[58] Locard believed that no matter where a person goes or what that person does, he will leave something at the scenes he visited. At the same time, he will also take something back with him from those places. A person at a crime scene can leave all sorts of evidence, including fingerprints, footprints, hair, skin, blood, bodily fluids, pieces of clothing, and more. By coming into contact with material at a crime scene, a criminal also takes part of that scene with him, whether it is dirt, hair, or any other type of trace evidence.

Prior to Locard's discoveries, physical evidence took a backseat to witness testimonies. In many parts of the world, superstition, squeamishness, and emotional respect for a deceased victim prevented investigators from performing invasive procedures like incisions, thereby limiting the amount of data they could collect.

Locard tested his principle during a 1912 murder case involving a young French woman named Marie Latelle. Latelle was found murdered in her

[58] http://science.howstuffworks.com/locards-exchange-principle1.htm

parents' home. Police questioned her boyfriend Emile Gourbin, who claimed he had been playing cards with some friends the night of the murder. When questioned, his friends confirmed Gourbin's alibi. But when Locard examined the corpse, he found evidence suggesting that Gourbin had lied. Locard first examined Latelle's body and found that she had been strangled. He then scraped underneath Emile Gourbin's fingernails for samples and viewed the results under a microscope. Locard noticed a pink dust among the samples, which he identified as ladies' makeup. He eventually located a chemist who produced the custom makeup Latelle had purchased. Locard discovered a match between the makeup Latelle had acquired and the samples coming from Gourbin's fingernails. When authorities confronted Gourbin with this evidence, he confessed to the murder. He had tricked his friends into believing his alibi by resetting the clock in their game room. Locard's exchange principle had worked.

As a result of the work of Bertillon and Locard, the presentation of physical evidence is now one of the most common occurrences in a court trial and has played a part in some of the most notable criminal trials. On March 1, 1932, Charles Lindbergh Jr., the 20-month old son of Charles Lindbergh, the famous aviator, was kidnapped. The elder Lindbergh is known for making the first solo nonstop flight across the Atlantic Ocean on May 20-21, 1927. The kidnapper climbed a ladder placed under the bedroom window of the child's room and snatched the infant by wrapping him in a blanket. The assailant left a note on the radiator in the child's room demanding a ransom of $50,000. The ransom was delivered, but the infant was never returned. Authorities discovered the child's body in May just a few miles from his home. Tracking the circulation of the bills used in the ransom payment led authorities to Bruno Hauptmann, who was found with over $14,000 of the money in his garage. Hauptmann claimed that the money belonged to a friend, but handwriting experts compared his writing to the script found on the ransom note and discovered them to be identical. Forensic analysts also connected wood found in Hauptmann's attic to the wood used in the make-shift ladder that the kidnapper built to reach the child's bedroom window. Hauptmann was convicted and executed in 1936, thanks to physical evidence.

George "Machine Gun" Kelly was a notorious gangster and bootlegger during the Prohibition era of the 1920s and early 1930s. His nickname came from the fact that his favorite weapon was a Thompson submachine gun.

On July 22, 1933, Kelly and his gang kidnapped Charles Urschel, a wealthy Oklahoma City oilman, and demanded a $200,000 ransom. Nine days later, after having received the ransom money, Kelly released Urschel unharmed. But during the ordeal, the oilman paid close attention to every detail and relayed it all to police. Though blindfolded, Urschel was able to distinguish day from night and kept track of such things as planes flying overhead, the day and time of thunderstorms, and the sounds of nearby farm animals. With these details, authorities were able to locate the farm where Kelly and his gang had been hiding. The vital link, however, was Charles Urschel's fingerprints, which he had placed on as many items in the farm house as possible. Based on the physical evidence provided by Urschel, the FBI arrested Kelly, and sentenced him to life in prison where he died in 1954. Again, physical evidence made the difference.

In addition to linking someone to a crime scene, physical evidence can also clear a person who has been wrongfully accused. Gerard Richardson of New Jersey served 19 years in prison for a murder he did not commit. Richardson was convicted in 1995 of murdering 19-year-old Monica Reyes, whose body was found in a ditch in Bernards Township in north-central New Jersey. The chief physical evidence included a bite mark on the victim's back that a prosecution expert said was made by Richardson. Although Richardson always maintained his innocence, earlier DNA testing of a swab of the bite mark was inconclusive. His attorneys eventually sought help from the Innocence Project, a non-profit national litigation and public policy organization dedicated to exonerating wrongfully convicted people through DNA testing. Attorneys at the Innocence Project took over Richardson's case and resubmitted the remaining evidence for testing. Forensics experts were able to extract a complete male DNA profile from the evidence, a profile that excluded Richardson. His exoneration came nearly two months after Somerset County Superior Court Judge Julie M. Marino overturned the conviction and ordered his release from prison.[59]

According to the Innocence Project, as of 2014, there have been 312 post-conviction DNA exonerations in the United States. The first DNA exoneration took place in 1989. Since then, exonerations have been won in 36 states.

[59] The Innocence Project
http://www.innocenceproject.org/Content/New_Jersey_Man_Exonerated_After_Serving_19_Years_for_a_Murder_that_New_DNA_Evidence_Shows_He_Didnt_Commit.php

Eighteen of the 312 people exonerated through DNA had been serving time on death row. Another 16 were charged with capital crimes but not sentenced to death. The average length of time served by exonerees is 13.5 years. The total number of years served is approximately 4,162. The average age of exonerees at the time of their wrongful convictions was 27. Races of the 312 exonerees were: 194 African Americans, 94 Caucasians, 22 Latinos, 2 Asian American. The true perpetrators have been identified in 153 of the DNA exoneration cases.[60] These statistics prove that the importance of physical evidence cannot be overstated.

In his Gospel, John presented physical evidence to prove that Jesus is the Christ, the son of God. He called these pieces of physical evidence "miraculous signs." For John, a miraculous sign was a supernatural feat that could only be performed by God. The fact that Jesus performed these miracles indicated that he is God. At first, John labeled these signs as the "beginning of signs" or "the second sign." After the second miraculous sign, John stopped counting them, but it is still easy to identify the pieces of physical evidence John presented. In all, John presented eight miraculous signs, but, like a good lawyer with a flair for the dramatic, he saved the best physical evidence for last. Concerning these signs and the people who witnessed them, Alyce M. McKenzie, a professor of homiletics at Southern Methodist University, noted that:

> Each of the signs reveals something about the human condition, ourselves in particular. They invite us to take on the role of the people Jesus encounters in each case. Many scholars believe this is why, in several cases, these people remain unnamed. The man by the pool, the boy at the feeding of the 5,000, the Galilean official and his son, the blind man—these people all presumably had names. But we will never know what they were. We are to fill in the blank with our own name. It may well be that John leaves them unnamed to make it easier for listeners to step into their space to stand with them in the experience of the scene.[61]

Here we will present the first seven miraculous signs.

---

[60]http://www.innocenceproject.org/Content/DNA_Exonerations_Nationwide.php
[61] http://www.patheos.com/Progressive-Christian/Wedding-Mishaps-Alyce-McKenzie-01-14-2013.html

First piece of physical evidence –
Jesus turned water into wine at a wedding in Cana of Galilee. (John 2:1-11)

Jesus' first and arguably his most well-known miracle was turning water into wine. John chapter two tells us that Jesus performed this miracle at a wedding feast in the Galilean village of Cana, nine miles northwest of Nazareth.

> On the third day a wedding took place at Cana in Galilee. Jesus' mother was there, and Jesus and his disciples had also been invited to the wedding. When the wine was gone, Jesus' mother said to him, "They have no more wine."
>
> "Woman, why do you involve me?" Jesus replied. "My hour has not yet come."
>
> But his mother said to the servants, "Do whatever he tells you."
>
> Nearby stood six stone water jars, the kind used by the Jews for ceremonial washing, each holding from twenty to thirty gallons. Jesus said to the servants, "Fill the jars with water"; so they filled them to the brim. Then he told them, "Now draw some out and take it to the master of the banquet."
>
> They did so, and the master of the banquet tasted the water that had been turned into wine. He did not realize where it had come from, though the servants who had drawn the water knew. Then he called the bridegroom aside and said, *"Everyone brings out the choice wine first and then the cheaper wine after the guests have had too much to drink; but you have saved the best till now."*
>
> What Jesus did here in Cana of Galilee was the first of the signs through which he revealed his glory; and his disciples believed in him.[62]

Having presided over a number of wedding ceremonies, I have seen some interesting circumstances take place. I've witnessed people faint, families refusing to speak to each other, rings lost, unity candles gone awry, to name a few. I was palm-sweating nervous at the first wedding ceremony I conducted. For one, the wedding was held in a different church from the one where I was pastor. Second, the church was the largest in our area, and it was expected to be packed. I rehearsed the ceremony over and over in my mind and in front of my bathroom mirror. I wanted to get it right. True to expectations, the day of the ceremony came with a packed sanctuary. I

[62] John 2:1-11

carefully and flawlessly worked my way through the ceremony until the end when, just after I presented the couple as husband and wife, and they were descending the platform steps, we all realized I had forgotten to have the groom kiss his bride. How on earth could I forget that? The couple wound up kissing part of the way down the aisle. Talk about being embarrassed!

Another embarrassing situation developed at the wedding feast Jesus attended in Cana. Along with Jesus were his disciples (John does not tell us how many at this point). Jesus' mother attended, whose name we are never told by John. She appears only twice in his Gospel, here at the wedding at Cana (John 2:1-11) and in chapter 19 where she stood by the cross and was entrusted by Jesus to the care of the Beloved Disciple (John 19:25-27). Interestingly, these two cameo appearances of Jesus' mother connect Jesus' first sign and his last breath.

The first century Jewish wedding consisted of a procession in which the groom brought the bride from her parents' home to his house, followed by a wedding feast. The festivities traditionally lasted seven days. Accommodating guests for such a lengthy celebration required a generous amount of lodging, food, and drink. Inadequate provisions would not only prove embarrassing, bringing the celebrations to a screeching halt, but also expose the families involved to legal liability. To the chagrin of the wedding director, the reception wine ran out. Jesus' mother reported the problem to Jesus, who seemed reluctant to do anything. Without requesting that Jesus do anything specific, his mother implied that she wanted him to do something and that she believed he could solve this problem. Her persistence prompted him to act. At the feast were six stone water pots used by the Jews for ceremonial washing. Each water pot could hold thirty gallons. Jesus instructed the servants to fill the pots with water, which Jesus then turned to wine. Afterward, Jesus directed the servants to take the wine to the wedding director for tasting. When the director of the feast tasted the wine, he was surprised and, I'm sure, elated.

Interestingly, few people even knew a miracle had taken place. Jesus, of course, knew; his mother most likely knew; the servants knew; and the disciples realized something special had happened because John says the miracle resulted in them believing in Jesus. Other than these, no one was aware. No lightning bolt cracked to herald the event. God's ways are not always on public display. As Lutheran pastor Roy Harrisville observed:

> God's glory is not what humans expect it to be. His glory is not for mere display, but has the purpose to fulfill his service to his creation. He buries Himself in a quiet tomb to do his work on Easter where no one can see or hear. As Martin Luther said, "God hides his pearls in a pile of dung so the devil can't find them."[63]

At the conclusion of the story, John added that "what Jesus did here in Cana of Galilee was the first of the signs through which he revealed his glory."[64] By making this statement, John clearly presented this event as physical evidence for Jesus' uniqueness.

The story yields many important truths. It is not insignificant that the entire tone of the wedding celebration changed from embarrassment to exhilaration the moment Jesus went from being a mere guest to acting as the host of the festivities. The fact that this sign occurred at a wedding suggests that a secret to long-lasting and meaningful marriages is for couples to recognize Jesus as the Lord of their relationship rather than a mere participant.

Assuming John would call the wedding director to testify in the case for Jesus, part of the man's testimony would consist of his words to the bridegroom in verse 10. His complete testimony might resemble the following:

John:	Sir, you are a wedding director, is that correct?
Wedding Director:	Yes, I am.
John:	Were you the director at a wedding in Cana near Galilee, a wedding Jesus attended?
Wedding Director:	I was.
John:	Something embarrassing happened at the wedding feast. What was it?
Wedding Director:	I am ashamed to say that we ran out of the wine for the reception. We thought we had ordered enough, but we ran out.
John:	So the wine ran out, and you had no more wine in storage.

[63] http://www.workingpreacher.org/profile/default.aspx?uid=2-harrisville_roy
[64] John 2:11

Wedding Director:	None at all!
John:	But in addition to the wine running out, something surprising occurred, is that right? What happened?
Wedding Director:	Yes. Not long after we realized the wine was gone, one of the servants came up to me with a flask of wine for me to taste. I tasted it. It was clearly a very fine wine, some of the best I have ever tasted.
John:	Where did this wine come from?
Wedding Director:	At the time, I did not know.
John:	Can you tell the court who is normally responsible for providing the wine at a wedding feast?
Wedding Director:	The bridegroom and his family.
John:	And did you ask the bridegroom about the wine?
Wedding Director:	Yes. I told him, "Everyone brings out the choice wine first and then the cheaper wine after the guests have had too much to drink; but you have saved the best till now."
John:	And what did the groom say?
Wedding Director:	He had no idea what I was talking about, nor did he know where the wine had come from!
John:	Did you ever find out where the wine came from?
Wedding Director:	My servants confided to me that this man Jesus provided it; that he somehow turned water from the stone washing pots into fine wine!
John:	So, it was Jesus who somehow miraculously provided this wine?
Wedding Director:	Yes, sir, it was. At least, that was what I was told.
John:	No further questions, sir.

Judge: Prosecution's witness!

Prosecutor Shaytan Kakos: Thank you, your Honor. Sir, you said that the bridegroom and his family are the ones normally responsible for providing wine at the reception. But they hired you to make sure this was taken care of so that they did not have to worry about it, is that not correct?

Wedding Director: Well, yes but—

Prosecutor Shaytan Kakos: Did you not agree to supervise the wedding feast?

Wedding Director: Yes, I did.

Prosecutor Shaytan Kakos: And were you not paid to do so?

Wedding Director: I was.

Prosecutor Shaytan Kakos: Are you aware—I'm sure you are!—that running out of food and drinks at the wedding feast is a serious crime for which the people responsible could be charged and even imprisoned?

Wedding Director: I am. But—

Prosecutor Shaytan Kakos: So by your testimony today you are incriminating not only yourself, but also the family that was kind enough to hire you. Did you even think about this before you took the stand today?

Wedding Director: Well, I thought since everything turned out okay, maybe—

Prosecutor Shaytan Kakos: Well, maybe you should think again! After all, there could be some serious repercussions! No further questions, your Honor.

Second piece of physical evidence –
Jesus healed the son of a royal official. (John 4:43-54)

The second miraculous sign noted by John was Jesus' long distance healing of a royal official's son.

> After the two days he left for Galilee. (Now Jesus himself had pointed out that a prophet has no honor in his own country.) When he arrived in Galilee, the Galileans welcomed him. They had seen all that he had done in Jerusalem at the Passover Festival, for they also had been there. Once more he visited Cana in Galilee, where he had turned the water into wine. And there was a certain royal official whose son lay sick at Capernaum. When this man heard that Jesus had arrived in Galilee from Judea, he went to him and begged him to come and heal his son, who was close to death.
>
> "Unless you people see signs and wonders," Jesus told him, "you will never believe."
>
> The royal official said, "Sir, come down before my child dies."
>
> "Go," Jesus replied, "your son will live."
>
> The man took Jesus at his word and departed. While he was still on the way, his servants met him with the news that his boy was living. When he inquired as to the time when his son got better, they said to him, "Yesterday, at one in the afternoon, the fever left him."
>
> Then the father realized that this was the exact time at which Jesus had said to him, "Your son will live." So he and his whole household believed.
>
> This was the second sign Jesus performed after coming from Judea to Galilee.[65]

As I examine this text, I cannot help but think of Bonnie Chester. Bonnie and her husband Cary are members of our church. They have no children together, but they both have children from previous marriages. Bonnie had one child, a son, named Austin Massey. When Austin was born on Friday, October 28, 1988, no one in his family could have predicted the impact he would have on every person he came in contact with. Austin had cancer from the time he was a baby, and it haggled him his entire life. He would beat it, and then it would come back, beat it, and then it would come

[65] John 4:43-54

back again. As a teenager, Austin loved University of Georgia football, fishing, hunting, four-wheeling, "muddin'," playing poker with his buddies, watching movies, hanging out with friends, worshipping with his youth group, and listening to music. A modified version of the 23rd Psalm aptly describes Austin and his love for the Georgia Bulldogs.

I am the Lord's bulldog; I do not like to lose.
He makes me to lie down on the 50 yard line;
He leads me into victorious end zones;
He restores my soul.
He leads me between the hedges of righteousness
for his name's sake.
Yea, though I walk through Death Valley, I will fear no evil,
For you are with me; your high fives and
Your staff they comfort me.
You prepare a table before me in the presence
of Gator fans;
You anoint my head with a helmet;
My Volunteer friends and my Tiger friends and
My Yellow Jacket friends get runneth over.
Surely red and black shall follow me all the days of my life,
And I will dwell between the hedges
Of the stadium of the Lord forever.[66]

Austin Massey died on Wednesday, May 20, 2009, at the age of 20. Austin was a renegade with a heart that bled for people. Those who knew Austin describe him as a fighter, a survivor, and a champion. His mom calls him her hero. The marker at his grave says, "MY SON, MY HERO, MY FRIEND." So many people attended his memorial service that we had to change the venue to a church large enough to accommodate the crowd. And even then, the service was standing room only. At a time when the average person's life expectancy reached 28,653 days, Austin's days numbered 7,509.[67] On most of those days, Bonnie Chester cried, prayed, and begged for God to heal her son. We prayed with her as well. For a time, after Austin died, his mother privately burned with anger. Though she still grieves for Austin, she now says that God did heal Austin, but in a different

[66] From the Memorial Service for Austin Massey, Saturday, May 23, 2009, 3:00 p.m. at Ramah First Baptist Church, Palmetto, Georgia.
[67] Elizabeth Arias, Ph.D., Division of Vital Statistics. National Vital Statistics Reports, Volume 62, Number 7, January 6, 2014, United States Life Tables, 2009. p. 1.

way than anyone expected. As much as anyone I know, Bonnie Chester knows what it feels like to be the Roman official whose son was at the point of death in John 4.

Bob Deffinbaugh also knows what it means to have a loved one's life in jeopardy. Deffinbaugh, a pastor in Richardson, Texas, relates:

> When I was 16 years old, my mother was seriously injured by a hit-and-run driver. I was the one driving her to the hospital, while my dad tried to stop the bleeding. When we reached the hospital, I rushed out of the car and into the hospital, where a lady on duty attempted to start filling out papers. I put an end to that quickly. I wanted help to save my mother's life, and I had no time for paper shuffling. Later in my life, my wife and I awoke to find our first child had died in his sleep. You can imagine my response when our next child appeared to be seriously ill. When I picked my daughter up, her eyes rolled to the back of her head. I did not care about speed limits that day; I only cared about getting help for her as quickly as possible. The royal official in [John 4] must feel the same way as his son's life hangs by a thread.[68]

John 4 tells us that the royal official rushed from Capernaum where he had taken his family to Cana of Galilee (about twenty miles) because he heard that Jesus was there. More important than being a royal official, this man was a father, and this father had one thing on his mind—getting Jesus to Capernaum as soon as possible, to save his son's life. The man evidently believed that Jesus could heal his son only if Jesus was by his son's side. Like Jesus' response to his mother in John 2:4, his response to this official was disturbingly brash.

> "Unless you people see signs and wonders," Jesus told him, "you will never believe."[69]

Furthermore, Jesus indicated that he would not be accompanying this desperate father back to Capernaum. Instead, Jesus told the man to go back home and that his son would live. The official did not get what he asked for; nevertheless, he believed Jesus and returned home. On his way, the

---

[68] https://bible.org/seriespage/jesus-heals-royal-official%E2%80%99s-son-john-443-54
[69] John 4:48

man was met by his servants with news of the boy's recovery. They did not want their master to worry any longer. When asked when the son began to recover, the servants confirmed that the time coincided with the moment Jesus told the man that his son would live.

At first, the nobleman incorrectly supposed that Jesus could only accomplish what he asked for by doing it the way the man prescribed. We all are like this at times when we pray. We tell God what we want, and then we proceed to tell him how to do it. We think that the way we expect God to act is the way he is most likely and able to act. The royal official assumed Jesus could save his son only if Jesus went to Capernaum to personally heal him. Jesus did intend to heal the man's son, but in his own way. He did not need to be at the boy's bedside.

John states in verse 54 that this was the second miraculous sign Jesus performed after he came from Judea to Galilee. As in the case of turning water to wine, John was intentional in listing this miracle as physical evidence in his case for Jesus. The testimony of the nobleman might look like the following:

John:	Sir, you are a royal official, correct?
Royal Official:	Yes, I serve as a courtier in the palace of King Herod Antipas.
John:	A courtier? And what does a courtier for Herod Antipas do?
Royal Official:	We tend to the King's wishes. Whatever the King needs, we provide. Whatever he commands us to do, we do it.
John:	You came to know Jesus because of a crisis in your family, right?
Royal Official:	Yes. My son was gravely ill at the time. His mother and I were told there was no cure. King Herod was kind enough to grant me leave so that my wife and I could seek out help for our son. She and I had taken him to every doctor we could find, hoping for a cure. I was desperate to save my son.

John: And so you went to see Jesus?

Royal Official: Yes. I was willing to do anything and try anything to save my son's life. At the time I heard about Jesus, my wife, my son, and I were in Capernaum, taking my son to doctors there, but my son was no better, rather he was getting worse. In fact, in Capernaum, he was too sick to travel. I heard that Jesus was some kind of miracle worker. I have little faith in miracle workers but, like I said, I was desperate. You would be too if your child were dying. As soon as I found out that Jesus was as close as Galilee, I knew I had to get to him before it was too late.

John: Tell us what happened when you located Jesus.

Royal Official: Once I discovered where Jesus was staying, I went straight there, asked for and found Jesus, and told him about the situation with my son. I told him that my son was dying, that I had heard he was a miracle worker, and that I needed him to come heal my son. I practically begged him to come. I told him I was desperate.

John: And how did Jesus respond? Did he go with you?

Royal Official: He did not. He wanted to argue about signs and wonders. He said, "Unless you people see signs and wonders, you will never believe."

John: And how did that make you feel?

Royal Official: Angry at first! Not that I was surprised that he initially resisted going with me. I

	assumed that he was somehow aware that I was a Herodian, and that he was suspicious of me on that account.
John:	Why would Jesus be suspicious of you as a Herodian?
Royal Official:	Well, some of my colleagues among the Herodians have not shown the kindest disposition toward Jesus.
John:	What do you mean?
Royal Official:	At one point, the Herodians teamed up with the Pharisees to oppose Jesus, although I was not part of that.
John:	Do the Herodians unite with the Pharisees often?
Royal Official:	Rarely. The Herodians and the Pharisees are usually on different sides of the political fence. The Pharisees dislike us because of our service to the Herod Dynasty.
John:	So the two groups rarely work together except when it comes to opposing Jesus. Is that correct?
Royal Official:	That is right.
John:	So for this reason, you were not initially surprised that Jesus was reluctant to accompany you to help your son.
Royal Official:	Yes, plus I did not expect him to immediately lay everything aside and go with me. Still, I was aggravated. I wanted him to be as urgent as I was. I said, "Sir, please! Come down before my son dies!"
John:	And then what did Jesus do?
Royal Official:	He told me to go home, that my son would live.
John:	Jesus did not just up and go with you?
Royal Official:	No, he did not.

John: You must have been disappointed that Jesus did not go with you; yet, in spite of this, you still believed him?

Royal Official: What choice did I have? I did not have the authority to force Jesus to go with me. I could have sent word asking my superiors to force Jesus to help me, but by that time, my son would have died. Anyway, I—I cannot really explain it, but somehow I did believe Jesus when he told me my son would live.

John: So what did you do?

Royal Official: At daybreak the next morning, I left to go back to Capernaum. On the way, some of my servants met me with the news that my boy had recovered. When I inquired as to the time when my son got better, they said to me, "Yesterday, at one in the afternoon, the fever left him." It was then I realized that this was the exact time at which Jesus had said to me, "Your son will live."

John: So your son was healed?

Royal Official: Yes, he was. He lives!

John: Before you went to Jesus, what did you believe about him?

Royal Official: Well, I did not know much of anything about him and, therefore, had formed no opinion of him. I had never met him. As I said before, I had heard about Jesus, about him performing miracles and the like.

John: Now that your son has recovered, what do you believe about Jesus?

Royal Official: I believe in him! Not only do I believe in him, but my entire family believes in

	him. I would follow him anywhere! He is my Lord!
John:	Thank you! No more questions.
Judge:	Does the prosecution wish to question the witness?
Prosecutor Shaytan Kakos:	Yes, your Honor. Sir, first, I want to say that I admire you for all you did for your son. I think any of us would have done the same for our children. You are certainly to be commended.
Royal Official:	Thank you.
Prosecutor Shaytan Kakos:	But, let me ask you (and please, I mean no disrespect in my question). Is it possible that your son might have recovered anyway? I mean, you have no proof that Jesus actually did anything that resulted in the recovery of your son, do you?
Royal Official:	All I can say is that my son became well at the same time Jesus said to me that he would live.
Prosecutor Shaytan Kakos:	Yes, but the fact that your son recovered at about the same time Jesus spoke to you does not prove with absolute certainty that Jesus healed your son, does it? Is it not possible that the timing of your son's healing and the timing of Jesus' statement could be nothing more than mere coincidence?
Royal Official:	Well, I suppose so, but—
Prosecutor Shaytan Kakos:	Yes, I suppose it could be coincidence, also. That is all I am saying, that at least there is the possibility that it could be mere coincidence. No more questions.

Third piece of physical evidence –
Jesus healed a paralyzed man at the pool of Bethesda. (John 5:1-9)

In his third miraculous sign in John, Jesus healed a man who had been paralyzed for almost forty years. Beginning with this sign, John stopped numbering the signs as he described them.

> Some time later, Jesus went up to Jerusalem for one of the Jewish festivals. Now there is in Jerusalem near the Sheep Gate a pool, which in Aramaic is called Bethesda and which is surrounded by five covered colonnades. Here a great number of disabled people used to lie—the blind, the lame, the paralyzed.[70]

John chapter 5 showed Jesus back in Jerusalem for an unnamed Jewish feast. Jesus stopped by the Pool of Bethesda, a pool fed by an underground spring surrounded by five porticoes. Legend had it that, at certain times, an angel would trouble the waters of the pool and then the first person into the water would be healed of whatever ailment they had.[71] First come, first served! Not surprisingly, the pool became the gathering place for people with all sorts of physical conditions, especially the blind, the lame, and the paralyzed. All gathered with eyes glued to the water for the smallest hint of rippling waves. A small bubbling from the underground spring or even the slightest breeze prompted a stampede of invalids vying to be the first into the water. No doubt, this pool was a place of much disappointment.

Another legend states that the Pool of Bethesda was used as a place where Asclepius, the Greek god of medicine and healing, cured his followers. Asclepius (also known as Serapis) was often pictured holding a staff with a snake around it. Archaeologists excavating the Pool of Bethesda have found several snake figures, possibly indicating that the area may have housed a Jerusalem branch of Asclepius cult. Some historians contend that the priests of Asclepius would drop snakes into the waters and proclaim healing for anyone who could step in.[72] The snakes' movement created the troubling of the waters mentioned in some versions of John 5.

---

[70] John 5:1-3

[71] This legend has been incorporated in verse 4 in some Bible versions (cf. King James Version), but it is not found in any New Testament manuscript written before the fourth century.

[72] Pool of Bethesda, Jerusalem: Jesus Heals the Paralytic, July 31, 2012 by Peter J. Fast http://peterjfast.com/2012/07/31/pool-of-bethesda-jerusalem-jesus-heals-the-paralytic/

Asclepius' mythical daughters included the goddesses Hygeia and Panacea. From their names, we get our modern words "hygiene" and "panacea," key concepts associated with medicine and health. Snakes were a key attribute of Asclepius' cult of health and healing. Even today, one of the key symbols of modern medicine is a stick surrounded by a snake. It is possible that the blind, lame, and paralyzed were not waiting for Israel's god to heal them, but rather for the merciful healing act of Asclepius.[73]

So Jesus went to Jerusalem on the Sabbath and visited a local landmark dedicated to the Greek god of healing, where he healed a man who had been paralyzed for 38 years. The writer Bruce Maples says:

> I don't know if [Jesus] was making a point about his power versus the power of other "gods." I don't know if he was making a point by choosing a man who had been lame 38 years. Nevertheless, I think there is a point here, and it is this: Sometimes, we sit and sit and sit, waiting for something magical to happen. The angel never appears, the water never stirs, and we are just as broken and just as powerless today as we were yesterday. Asclepius, that false god, has let us down again. Then Jesus reaches out to us, and our waiting is over, and our healing begins. And this is the sign, the point I believe Jesus is making: Jesus brings life, while everything else just brings waiting.[74]

It was here that Jesus healed the paralyzed man. The paralytic came to the pool with the hopes of being the first to make it into the water.

> One who was there had been an invalid for thirty-eight years. When Jesus saw him lying there and learned that he had been in this condition for a long time, he asked him, "Do you want to get well?"
>
> *"Sir," the invalid replied, "I have no one to help me into the pool when the water is stirred. While I am trying to get in, someone else goes down ahead of me."*

---

[73] Who Will Heal You? A Greek or a Jewish god? (John 5:2-5), Jewish Studies for Christians: Official Blog of Dr. Eli Lizorkin-Eyzenberg. http://jewishstudies.eteacherbiblical.com/john-5-2-5-who-will-heal-you-a-greek-or-a-jewish-god/

[74] http://brucewriter.com/waiting-to-be-healed-a-lection-reflection-on-john-5/

> Then Jesus said to him, "Get up! Pick up your mat and walk." At once the man was cured; he picked up his mat and walked. [75]

Because the man was no stranger to the pool, many people knew his story. Jesus asked him, "Do you want to be made whole? Do you want to get well?" Instead of a simple "yes," the man played the blame game, accusing some people of refusing to help him into the water, and accusing others of beating him to the water. It is possible that the man had grown accustomed to the attention he received from being an invalid and therefore did not want to be healed. Jesus addressed neither the man's accusations nor his motives, but rather cut to the root of the man's problem by ordering the man to get up, pick up his mat, and walk. The man stood up, picked up his mat, and walked…for the first time in thirty-eight years!

John tells us that Jesus healed the man on the Sabbath, the Jewish holy day which ran from Friday at 6:00 p.m. until Saturday at 6:00 p.m. It was forbidden by Jewish Law for a person to heal another person on the Sabbath. It was also illegal for a man to carry his mat on the Sabbath.

> The day on which this took place was a Sabbath, and so the Jews said to the man who had been healed, "It is the Sabbath; the law forbids you to carry your mat." But he replied, "*The man who made me well said to me, 'Pick up your mat and walk.'*" So they asked him, "Who is this fellow who told you to pick it up and walk?" The man who was healed had no idea who it was, for Jesus had slipped away into the crowd that was there. Later Jesus found him at the temple and said to him, "See, you are well again. Stop sinning or something worse may happen to you." *The man went away and told the Jewish leaders that it was Jesus who had made him well.*[76]

When the Jewish leaders caught the man carrying his mat, they questioned him. The man blamed Jesus, although he did not know Jesus' name. Jesus later found the man in the temple, whereupon the man learned Jesus' name and forthwith reported to the leaders that Jesus had healed him.

John's questioning of this man could be described as follows:

---

[75] John 5:5-9a
[76] John 5:9-15

John: Sir, is it true that, for most of your life, you have been an invalid, unable to walk? Is that correct?

The Man: Yes, for thirty-eight years.

John: During that time, did you ever go to the Pool of Bethesda?

The Man: Someone carried me to the pool almost every day.

John: Please tell the court why you went to the Pool of Bethesda.

The Man: Because, at times, an angel comes down to the pool, troubles the waters, and then the first person into the pool is healed of whatever disease or infirmity he has.

John: So you came to the pool in hopes of being healed so you could walk?

The Man: Yes, sir, I did.

John: Thirty-eight years! You must have experienced a lot of disappointment coming to that pool year after year, but leaving in the same shape in which you came. Yes?

The Man: A lot of disappointment, yes.

John: Have you ever seen the defendant at the pool?

The Man: Yes, he came by one day while I was waiting at the pool.

John: Did he talk to you?

The Man: He did.

John: And what did Jesus say to you?

The Man: He asked me if I wanted to be well.

John: And did you want to get well?

The Man: Of course, I wanted to get well! Why do you think I went to the pool in the first place? I assure you I did not go there for the attention!

John:	Very well, then, what was your response to him?
The Man:	Well, for one thing, I never had anyone to put me into the water. And someone else always beat me to the water.
John:	What did Jesus say next?
The Man:	He just told me to stand up, pick up my mat, and leave.
John:	What happened next?
The Man:	I stood up, as the man told me, gathered my mat, and left.
John:	Then what happened?
The Man:	The city leaders confronted me because I was carrying my mat on the Sabbath day. I told them the man who made me well said to me, "Pick up your mat and walk." But, at the time, I did not know the man's name.
John:	So they asked you for his name?
The Man:	Yes, but I did not know his name.
John:	But later, you saw Jesus again, and found out his name.
The Man:	I saw him later that day in the Temple, and learned that his name was Jesus.
John:	Did you report back to the leaders?
The Man:	Yes, I told them Jesus was the one who healed me.
John:	So, after thirty-eight years of being paralyzed, you are telling us that Jesus Christ healed you?
The Man:	Yes, Jesus made me well.

The prosecutor's cross-examination of the man comes from questions the religious leaders asked him in John chapter 5.

Asst. Prosecutor Ray Scotia:	Sir, are you a religious man?

The Man:	Yes. Well, I try to be. I have to admit that I have not been able to attend synagogue much because of my handicap, but I believe in God, the Law and the Prophets.
Asst. Prosecutor Ray Scotia:	I appreciate that. I too am a religious man. I believe in God. Well, since you are a religious man and you read the Law, I am sure you are aware of what the Sabbath day is, sir. Correct?
The Man:	Well, I am certainly no expert on the Law, but I believe the Sabbath is the day of the week when we are to rest and worship.
Asst. Prosecutor Ray Scotia:	And do you know who it was that gave us the Sabbath day?
The Man:	No, I do not. I suppose the religious leaders, perhaps the Pharisees or Sadducees, gave it to us. Not sure.
Asst. Prosecutor Ray Scotia:	What would you say if I told you that God himself gave us the Sabbath day?
The Man:	Oh! I was not aware of that.
Asst. Prosecutor Ray Scotia:	You do believe in God, do you not? Being a religious man and all?
The Man:	Oh, absolutely!
Asst. Prosecutor Ray Scotia:	Well, then, the God you and I believe in is the one who gave us the Sabbath. And do you know *why* God gave us the Sabbath, sir?
The Man:	Uh…I guess, to worship him, maybe? I don't know.
Asst. Prosecutor Ray Scotia:	God gave us the Sabbath as a day of rest because the Torah tells us that God himself rested on the seventh day, the Sabbath day, when he created the world. Surely you knew that, right?
The Man:	I am sure I did, but I forgot.

Asst. Prosecutor Ray Scotia: As a matter of fact, sir, not only was God the one who gave us the Sabbath, and not only did God himself rest on the Sabbath day, but God told us to remember the Sabbath day, to keep the Sabbath day holy, and to rest on the Sabbath. Now, in light of the fact that our Sabbath day came from God, and that the laws that govern the Sabbath came from God, how important do you think the Sabbath day is?

The Man: Very important!

Asst. Prosecutor Ray Scotia: I would agree! The Sabbath is very important! Now, sir, do you think a person, any person, could be led by God to do away with or to outright violate the very Sabbath laws God himself put in place?

The Man: No, sir, I guess not.

Asst. Prosecutor Ray Scotia: Sir, do you honestly believe that a person who blatantly disobeys and disregards God's Sabbath law could legitimately claim to be sent by God?

The Man: No, sir, I guess not. I do not see how that could be.

Asst. Prosecutor Ray Scotia: Of course not! That would not make sense now, would it?

The Man: No, sir.

Asst. Prosecutor Ray Scotia: But yet, Jesus supposedly healed you on, let me see, what day was it?

The Man: Uh…the Sabbath.

Asst. Prosecutor Ray Scotia: The Sabbath day! Jesus claims to have healed people on the very day God said to rest and worship! Now you have already stated here that you cannot see how such a man as Jesus who arrogantly and irreverently and

	repeatedly disregards God's Sabbath could possibly be sent from God. So Jesus could not possibly be sent from God, could he, sir?
The Man:	Well, I—! Look, all I know is that this man helped me to walk for the first time in my life. So, I just cannot bring myself to criticize Jesus—
Asst. Prosecutor Ray Scotia:	You do know, do you not, sir, that the Law of Moses forbids you to carry your mat on the Sabbath?
The Man:	Pardon me?
Asst. Prosecutor Ray Scotia:	I asked you whether you are aware that the Law of Moses forbids you to carry your mat on the Sabbath.
The Man:	Well, I, no, I did not know that.
Asst. Prosecutor Ray Scotia:	Well, it is true! Anyone who carries his mat on the Sabbath day is in direct violation of the Law of God handed down to Moses by God himself. So, I suggest, sir that you think long and hard about your answers in court today. Now I will ask you again: Is it really possible that a man such as Jesus, who arrogantly and irreverently and repeatedly disregards God's Sabbath, could possibly be sent from God? Surely you do not think it is possible!
The Man:	Well, I never thought of it that way. I—I guess not.
Asst. Prosecutor Ray Scotia:	I guess not, too! Thank you. No further questions for this witness, your Honor.

Fourth piece of physical evidence –
Jesus fed over five thousand people with five barley loaves and two fish. (John 6:1-15)

The feeding of the five thousand is the only miracle story recounted in all four Gospels.

> Some time after this, Jesus crossed to the far shore of the Sea of Galilee (that is, the Sea of Tiberias), and a great crowd of people followed him because they saw the signs he had performed by healing the sick. Then Jesus went up on a mountainside and sat down with his disciples. The Jewish Passover Festival was near. When Jesus looked up and saw a great crowd coming toward him, he said to Philip, "Where shall we buy bread for these people to eat?" He asked this only to test him, for he already had in mind what he was going to do.
>
> Philip answered him, "It would take more than half a year's wages to buy enough bread for each one to have a bite!"
>
> Another of his disciples, Andrew, Simon Peter's brother, spoke up, "Here is a boy with five small barley loaves and two small fish, but how far will they go among so many?"
>
> Jesus said, "Have the people sit down." There was plenty of grass in that place, and they sat down (about five thousand men were there). Jesus then took the loaves, gave thanks, and distributed to those who were seated as much as they wanted. He did the same with the fish. When they had all had enough to eat, he said to his disciples, "Gather the pieces that are left over. Let nothing be wasted." So they gathered them and filled twelve baskets with the pieces of the five barley loaves left over by those who had eaten.
>
> After the people saw the sign Jesus performed, they began to say, "Surely this is the Prophet who is to come into the world." Jesus, knowing that they intended to come and make him king by force, withdrew again to a mountain by himself.[77]

John stated that five thousand men were present when Jesus performed this miracle. In keeping with the cultural traditions of the day, John did not include women and children in his numbering. Assuming that women and children were also present, the actual total may well have reached between

---

[77] John 6:1-15

ten and fifteen thousand. By multiplying bread to feed these people, Jesus did more than merely satisfy their hunger pangs.

New Testament professor Brian Peterson notes the strong connection between Jesus and Moses in this text. He says:

> At the end of chapter 5, Jesus complained that his opponents did not understand or believe what Moses had written (John 5:39-47). We then are ushered immediately into a scene that not only takes place at Passover, one of the great events associated with Moses, but into a text that overflows with echoes of the Passover event. Some examples include:
>
> - At the beginning of chapter 6, events of supernatural feeding and of salvation from the sea are joined together, just as the crossing of the sea and the manna in the wilderness were part of the story of Moses.
> - There is "testing" here (John 6:6), as there was in Exodus 16:4.
> - Jesus commands that the pieces be gathered up so that nothing is wasted, just as Moses commanded in Exodus 16:19.
> - Jesus is said to go up "on a mountainside." In fact, the text strangely says that after the feeding, Jesus (again?) withdrew "to a mountain" (verse 15). Perhaps this repeated mention of "a mountain" (another piece unique to John's account) is intended to recall that other mountain in Israel's story, where Moses met God.
> - The people will grumble (verse 41), just as Israel did in the wilderness (Exodus 16:2).
>
> Thus, this text is an echo chamber of the Passover-Exodus story. If chapter 5 ended with complaints about a shallow, superficial understanding of Moses, then chapter 6 intends to show a deeper, fuller understanding of Moses and the Passover which is now revealed in Jesus.[78]

Jesus provided bread in a mysterious way to a group of hungry people in a remote area, thereby meeting their physical needs. On one level, he was serving as the prophet like Moses who the people expected, and who

[78] http://www.workingpreacher.org/preaching.aspx?commentary_id=350.

himself miraculously provided food to an earlier group of people in a remote land. On another level, the bread symbolized the fact that Jesus himself is the bread "from heaven" that satisfies the spiritual need of every human being.

Fifth piece of physical evidence –
Jesus walked on water on the Sea of Galilee. (John 6:16-21)

The fifth miraculous sign John recorded was Jesus walking on the Sea of Galilee in the midst of a grueling storm. This miracle is recorded in three of the Gospels (Matthew 14:22-36; Mark 6:45-56; John 6:16-21), and comes on the heels of the feeding of the five thousand.

> When evening came, his disciples went down to the lake, where they got into a boat and set off across the lake for Capernaum. By now it was dark, and Jesus had not yet joined them. A strong wind was blowing and the waters grew rough. When they had rowed about three or four miles, they saw Jesus approaching the boat, walking on the water; and they were frightened. But he said to them, "It is I; don't be afraid." Then they were willing to take him into the boat, and immediately the boat reached the shore where they were heading.[79]

By walking on the water, Jesus proved himself to be in command of the elements of nature, something only God can do, and he convinced his disciples that he was indeed the Son of God.[80] In placing this event where he did, John further tied Jesus to Moses in that, whereas Moses was instrumental in parting the Red Sea[81], Jesus exercised more power than Moses by walking on top of the sea.

Sixth piece of physical evidence –
Jesus gave sight to a blind man. (John 9)

> As he went along, he saw a man blind from birth. His disciples asked him, "Rabbi, who sinned, this man or his parents, that he was born blind?"

[79] John 6:16-21.

[80] See also Matthew 14:32-33.

[81] Exodus 14.

> "Neither this man nor his parents sinned," said Jesus, "but this happened so that the works of God might be displayed in him. As long as it is day, we must do the works of him who sent me. Night is coming, when no one can work. While I am in the world, I am the light of the world."
>
> After saying this, he spit on the ground, made some mud with the saliva, and put it on the man's eyes. "Go," he told him, "wash in the Pool of Siloam" (this word means "Sent"). So the man went and washed, and came home seeing.
>
> His neighbors and those who had formerly seen him begging asked, "*Isn't this the same man who used to sit and beg?*" Some claimed that he was.
>
> Others said, "*No, he only looks like him.*"
>
> But he himself insisted, "*I am the man.*"[82]

In John chapter 9, Jesus gave sight to a man who was born blind. Jesus took the unusual measure of spitting on the ground, making mud with his spit, and smearing the mud on the man's eyes. Jesus then instructed the man to wash his face in the Pool of Siloam, a pool located on the south side of ancient Jerusalem in what is known as the City of David. During the time of Jesus, the poor and the sick went to the pool to bathe. The man went to the pool, bathed in the water, and gained his sight. This event is Jesus' sixth miracle in John. John interspersed the story amid an extended debate between Jesus and the religious leaders in which the latter sought to refute Jesus' claims to have been sent by God. John sandwiched the story of the blind man in the middle of this debate to showcase the blindness of the religious leaders, the very ones who should have known who Jesus was.

John wrote the interaction in chapter 9 in such a way that the questions posed by the blind man's neighbors and acquaintances as well as the questions posed by the religious leaders most naturally fit the questions that the prosecuting attorney would ask in a courtroom. The courtroom dialogue could flow as follows:

Prosecutor Shaytan Kakos:	How are you today, sir?
Blind Man:	I am doing well, thank you.
Prosecutor Shaytan Kakos:	How is your eyesight? Are you able to see me clearly?
Blind Man:	Oh yes, quite clearly!

---

[82] John 9:1-9.

Prosecutor Shaytan Kakos:	Excellent! I am glad to hear that. Tell me, how easy is it to pretend like you are blind?
Blind Man:	Pardon me?
Prosecutor Shaytan Kakos:	Are you not the same man who used to sit and beg, acting as though you were blind? Was that not you?
Blind Man:	I was not pretending that I was blind. I was blind, and it is true, I used to sit and beg.
Prosecutor Shaytan Kakos:	Why not just tell the truth? You are *not* the same man. The truth is you have *never* been blind. You were only trying to appear as though you were blind.
Blind Man:	That is not true!
Prosecutor Shaytan Kakos:	In reality, you are not the man who was blind, are you?
Blind Man:	I am the man!
Prosecutor Shaytan Kakos:	How then were your eyes opened?
Blind Man:	The man they call Jesus made some mud and put it on my eyes. He told me to go to the Pool of Siloam and wash. So I went and washed, and then I could see.
Prosecutor Shaytan Kakos:	So this man Jesus daubed mud in your eyes? Is this really the way someone who is sent from God goes about giving sight to the blind, by daubing mud in that person's eyes? Does that really sound like a person sent by God?
Blind Man:	Well, I will have to admit that it was a bit unorthodox, but that is the way he did it.
Prosecutor Shaytan Kakos:	Does that really sound like a godly man to you? It sounds more like a devil to me! What have you to say about him? It was your eyes he opened! What do you make of him?

Blind Man:	I say he is a prophet.
Prosecutor Shaytan Kakos:	You expect us to believe that you were blind and then received your sight because someone smeared mud and spit in your eyes? Have you ever heard of that happening to anyone? That has never happened to anyone! And yet you expect us to believe that this man gave you sight? It sure looks to me, sir, that you are still more blind than you realize!
John:	Objection, your Honor! Counsel is badgering the witness.
Prosecutor Shaytan Kakos:	Withdrawn.

Later, the prosecutor cross-examined the blind man's parents.

Prosecutor Shaytan Kakos:	Is this your son? *(Pointing to the man.)*
Parents:	Yes, he is our son.
Prosecutor Shaytan Kakos:	Is this man the same one you say was born blind?
Parents:	Yes, he has been blind all his life.
Prosecutor Shaytan Kakos:	How is it that now he can see?
Parents:	How he can see now, or who opened his eyes, we do not know. We only know that—
Prosecutor Shaytan Kakos:	In reality, this man not only is not your son, but he has never been blind. Is that not the truth?
Parents:	We know he is our son, and we know he was born blind. But—
Prosecutor Shaytan Kakos:	Well, tell us, then, in front of this jury and this distinguished host of religious leaders present, do you really believe what this man claims, that the man called Jesus gave him his sight?

Parents:	As we have already said, how he can see now, or who opened his eyes, we do not know.
Prosecutor Shaytan Kakos:	Then how is it that now he can see?
Parents:	We don't know. Ask him. He is old enough to speak for himself!

After getting nowhere with the parents of the blind man, the prosecutor recalled the blind man to the witness stand.

Prosecutor Shaytan Kakos:	You say you were blind, but now you see. If this is true, then give credit to God for your sight! As for this man, Jesus, we know what he is. We know he is a sinner!
Blind Man:	Look! Whether he is a sinner or not, I do not know, but one thing I do know: I was blind but now I see!
Prosecutor Shaytan Kakos:	What did he do to you? How did he open your eyes?
Blind Man:	I have told you already and you won't listen. Why do you want to hear it again? Do you want to become his disciple, too?
Prosecutor Shaytan Kakos:	I will be the one to ask the questions, sir! You just answer them! You obviously are one of this fellow's disciples, lying on his behalf! We, on the other hand, are disciples of Moses! We know that God spoke to Moses, but as for this fellow, we do not even know where he comes from. So are you one of his disciples?
Blind Man:	Now that is remarkable! You say you do not know where he comes from, yet he opened my eyes. We both know that God does not listen to sinners.

Prosecutor Shaytan Kakos:	Sir—
Blind Man:	He listens to the godly man who does his will.
Prosecutor Shaytan Kakos:	Sir!
Blind Man:	Nobody has ever heard of opening the eyes of a man born blind. If this man were not from God, he would not have been able to do such a thing. But he obviously is from God. Had he not been from God, then he could have done nothing!
Prosecutor Shaytan Kakos:	So you too have fallen for his lies!
Blind Man:	No, I—
Prosecutor Shaytan Kakos:	No further questions, your Honor!
Judge:	Very well. Does the defense wish to question the witness?
John:	Yes, your Honor, just one question. Sir, you saw Jesus. Jesus enabled you to see. You talked with him. So, tell us, what is your opinion of him?
Blind Man:	Sir, I believe in him, and I worship him as my Lord.
John:	Thank you, sir. No further questions, your Honor.

Seventh piece of physical evidence –
Jesus raised Lazarus from the dead. (John 11:1-44)

Aside from the resurrection of Jesus, the most powerful miracle Jesus performed was the miracle of raising his friend Lazarus from the dead after Lazarus had been in the tomb four days. It is a story that, remarkably, is not found in any other Gospel.

Lazarus and his two sisters, Mary and Martha, were friends with Jesus. They lived in the village of Bethany, about two miles southeast of Jerusalem. All four Gospels record that Jesus often visited there, usually staying in the home of Lazarus and his sisters. According to John 11, when Lazarus fell terminally ill, his sisters sent word to Jesus, "Lord, the one you love is sick." Upon hearing the news, Jesus waited two more days before going to Lazarus' hometown of Bethany. When Jesus arrived in Bethany, Lazarus had already died and been in the tomb for four days. Jesus had missed the hospital visitation and the funeral.

> On his arrival, Jesus found that Lazarus had already been in the tomb for four days. Now Bethany was less than two miles from Jerusalem, and many Jews had come to Martha and Mary to comfort them in the loss of their brother. When Martha heard that Jesus was coming, she went out to meet him, but Mary stayed at home. "*Lord,*" Martha said to Jesus, "*if you had been here, my brother would not have died. But I know that even now God will give you whatever you ask.*"
>
> Jesus said to her, "Your brother will rise again."
>
> Martha answered, "*I know he will rise again in the resurrection at the last day.*"
>
> Jesus said to her, "I am the resurrection and the life. The one who believes in me will live, even though they die; and whoever lives by believing in me will never die. Do you believe this?"
>
> "Yes, Lord," she replied, "*I believe that you are the Messiah, the Son of God, who is to come into the world.*"
>
> After she had said this, she went back and called her sister Mary aside. "The Teacher is here," she said, "and is asking for you." When Mary heard this, she got up quickly and went to him. Now Jesus had not yet entered the village, but was still at the place where Martha had met him. When the Jews who had been with Mary in the house, comforting her, noticed how quickly she got up and went out, they followed her, supposing she was going to the tomb to mourn there.
>
> When Mary reached the place where Jesus was and saw him, she fell at his feet and said, "Lord, if you had been here, my brother would not have died."
>
> When Jesus saw her weeping, and the Jews who had come along with her also weeping, he was deeply moved in spirit and troubled. "Where have you laid him?" he asked.
>
> "Come and see, Lord," they replied.
>
> Jesus wept.
>
> Then the Jews said, "See how he loved him!"
>
> But some of them said, "Could not he who opened the eyes of the blind man have kept this man from dying?"

Jesus, once more deeply moved, came to the tomb. It was a cave with a stone laid across the entrance. "Take away the stone," he said.

"*But, Lord,*" said Martha, the sister of the dead man, "*by this time there is a bad odor, for he has been there four days.*"

Then Jesus said, "Did I not tell you that if you believe, you will see the glory of God?"

So they took away the stone. Then Jesus looked up and said, "Father, I thank you that you have heard me. I knew that you always hear me, but I said this for the benefit of the people standing here, that they may believe that you sent me." *When he had said this, Jesus called in a loud voice, "Lazarus, come out!" The dead man came out, his hands and feet wrapped with strips of linen, and a cloth around his face. Jesus said to them, "Take off the grave clothes and let him go.*"[83]

The dialogue below imagines testimony from Martha as she answers questions, first from John, and then from the assistant prosecuting attorney.

John:	Will you please state your name?
Martha:	Martha, from the town of Bethany. I am the sister of Lazarus and Mary.
John:	Martha, how well do you know Jesus?
Martha:	I know him very well. Jesus is a close friend of our family. Each time he came to Jerusalem, he stayed at our home in Bethany, a short walk from Jerusalem.
John:	Would you say that Jesus is among your family's closest friends?
Martha:	Yes, I would.
John:	Could you please tell the court what happened when your brother Lazarus became sick and then eventually died?
Martha:	When Lazarus became ill, Mary and I naturally thought he would get over his sickness in a few days. Instead, his condition worsened, and we became worried. So we sent for Jesus, who lived

[83] John 11:17-44

in Galilee. We told him that Lazarus, the one he loves, is sick. While we waited for Jesus to come, Lazarus died. When the time came for the funeral service, Jesus had still not arrived. So we went ahead with the funeral service, and placed Lazarus' body in the tomb.

John: Did Jesus ever show up?

Martha: He did, about four days after the memorial service.

John: What happened then?

Martha: When Jesus arrived, I went out to meet him. I told him that my brother Lazarus had died, and that things might have turned out differently had he been there. Jesus then told me that Lazarus would rise again. I said that I know he will rise again in the resurrection at the last day. But then Jesus told me that he was the resurrection and the life, and that everyone who believes in him will live, even though they die; and that whoever believes in him will never die. Then he asked me if I believed what he was saying. I told him I did believe.

John: Then what happened?

Martha: I sent for Mary, my sister. She came out to meet Jesus. We all cried. He wept with us. Then he asked us to take him to the cemetery. When we got to the cemetery, other people were there, grieving over Lazarus' death. After a few minutes, Jesus told us to take away the stone from Lazarus' grave. I did not think this was a good idea. I told Jesus that by that time there would be a bad odor, for Lazarus had been in the tomb four days.

John: What happened next?

Martha: Jesus insisted that we remove the stone. So, some of the men took away the stone. Then Jesus looked up and appeared to be praying to God. Then he called in a loud voice, "Lazarus, come out!" All of a sudden, Lazarus came out, his hands and feet wrapped with strips of linen, and a cloth around his face. Jesus told us to take off Lazarus' grave clothes and let him go.

John: Are you telling us that Jesus raised Lazarus from the dead after Lazarus had been dead at least four days?

Martha: I would not have believed it had I not seen it with my own eyes. Yes, Jesus raised my brother from the dead!

John: So what do you believe about Jesus?

Martha: I believe that he is the Messiah, the Son of God, who was prophesied to come into the world.

John: Thank you, Martha. No further questions at this time.

Judge: Does the prosecution have any questions for Martha?

Asst. Prosecutor Paula Ponera: Yes, your Honor. Thank you. Martha, when your brother, Lazarus, became ill, you called for Jesus to come to his side, did you not?

Martha: Yes, we did.

Asst. Prosecutor Paula Ponera: While your brother was sick, when he was still living, did Jesus arrive?

Martha: Well…Jesus did arrive at—

Asst. Prosecutor Paula Ponera: My question was 'did Jesus arrive while your brother was still alive?'

Martha: No, not while Lazarus was alive.

Asst. Prosecutor Paula Ponera: But you obviously had hoped Jesus would come heal Lazarus of his sickness; is that a fair assumption?

Martha: That is the reason we sent for him.

Asst. Prosecutor Paula Ponera: But your brother did indeed die before Jesus arrived. In fact, as you have already stated, Jesus did not arrive until well after the funeral service, right?

Martha: Yes, but, you see—

Asst. Prosecutor Paula Ponera: I guess Jesus had more important things to do than be there for you in your time of intense grief.

John: Objection, your Honor! There is no question there.

Judge: Sustained.

Asst. Prosecutor Paula Ponera: Martha, who spoke at Lazarus' memorial service?

Martha: Who spoke?

Asst. Prosecutor Paula Ponera: Yes, who spoke at Lazarus' memorial service? Did any ministers or rabbis speak or offer a eulogy?

Martha: Well, uh, Mary and I tried to speak, and a local Rabbi from our village delivered a message.

Asst. Prosecutor Paula Ponera: But you preferred to have Jesus speak at Lazarus' funeral, did you not, Martha? But Jesus failed to show up, is that not right?

Martha: Well, I—

Asst. Prosecutor Paula Ponera: All I need is a yes or no, Martha! Is it not correct that Jesus failed to show up for the funeral service?

Martha: Yes, that is true, but—

Asst. Prosecutor Paula Ponera: Tell me, Martha, what kind of person is this Jesus, anyway? You sent word for him to come to the hospital, and he did

	not come; and you wanted him to speak at the funeral, but he did not show up for the funeral either. Now what kind of pastor would do that to someone he is supposed to love and care for?
Martha:	Uh, he is, Jesus is—
Asst. Prosecutor Paula Ponera:	Oh, that's all right, Martha, you do not have to answer that. No more questions, your Honor!

The people who witnessed Jesus raising Lazarus from the dead went about telling everyone what they had seen. John described the crowds' actions in John 12.

> Now the crowd that was with him when he called Lazarus from the tomb and raised him from the dead continued to spread the word. Many people, because they had heard that he had given this miraculous sign, went out to meet him. So the Pharisees said to one another, "See, this is getting us nowhere. Look how the whole world has gone after him!"[84]

Although John did not record what the people in the crowd said about Jesus raising Lazarus from the tomb, we can safely speculate how their testimonies might have sounded.

John:	Sir, you are friends with the family of Mary, Martha, and Lazarus?
Man:	Yes, sir, I am.
John:	Were you present when Jesus arrived at Lazarus' grave?
Man:	I was.
John:	What did you see?
Man:	I was standing on a hill several yards from the tomb. I could see Jesus talking to Martha and Mary. I could not hear what they were saying, but they were obviously saddened; they were still

[84] John 12:17-19

crying. Then some people removed the stone from the opening of the tomb. In a loud voice, Jesus called Lazarus to come out. I thought it was crazy. Next thing I knew, Lazarus came out!

John: Were there other people who saw Jesus perform this miracle?

Man: Oh, yes, lots of people were there.

John: Did you tell anyone what you saw?

Man: I'll say! We told everybody we met! Still are! Never seen anything like it!

John: Thank you, sir. No further questions, your Honor.

Judge: Does the prosecution wish to question the witness?

Asst. Prosecutor Ray Scotia: Yes, your Honor. Thank you. Sir, have you ever heard of the term 'coma' or heard of anyone being in a coma?

Man: I am sorry?

Asst. Prosecutor Ray Scotia: Have you ever heard of anyone being in a coma? Do you know what a coma is?

Man: No, I have never heard of anyone being in a coma. I have never heard that term.

Asst. Prosecutor Ray Scotia: Sir, a coma is when a person is unconscious for a prolonged period of time. While that person is in a coma, he is very much alive, but looks like he is sleeping or even dead. This state can last for as little as a few hours or as long as several years. A person in a coma does not respond to any kind of stimulation until he starts to awaken from the coma. Do you now understand what a coma is?

Man: Yes, I think I understand. I had never heard of it until now.

Asst. Prosecutor Ray Scotia: In light of what a coma is, do you think it is at least possible that your friend Lazarus was in a coma as opposed to being dead?

Man: So you are telling me that a person in what you are referring to as a coma actually looks dead, but is not dead?

Asst. Prosecutor Ray Scotia: That is exactly what I am saying. So, do you think it is at least possible that your friend Lazarus was in a coma as opposed to being dead?

Man: Well, I suppose so.

Asst. Prosecutor Ray Scotia: That Lazarus was in a coma certainly sounds more believable than to say that he had been dead four days, and then Jesus finally showed up and raised him from the dead, wouldn't you say?

Man: It would be easier to believe. Yes.

Asst. Prosecutor Ray Scotia: Yes, it would! That is all I am asking. Thank you. No further questions for this witness, your Honor.

From his seat, John surveyed the faces of the jurors. Some of the jurors nodded in agreement when Assistant Prosecutor Scotia suggested that Lazarus being in a coma was more credible than Jesus raising him from the dead after four days. John could see that the jurors were not yet convinced of Jesus' true identity. He still had work to do to fully convince them of who Jesus really was. As part of John's continuing defense of Jesus, he reserved the eighth and final piece of physical evidence for last.

6 Enlisting an Expert Witness to Testify

An intelligent evaluation of facts is often difficult or impossible without the testimonies of people with scientific, technical, or other specialized knowledge. According to the Cornell University Law Information Institute, a witness who is qualified as an expert by knowledge, skill, experience, training, or education may testify in the form of an opinion or otherwise if:

> (a) the expert's scientific, technical, or other specialized knowledge will help the trier of fact to understand the evidence or to determine a fact in issue; (b) the testimony is based on sufficient facts or data; (c) the testimony is the product of reliable principles and methods; and (d) the expert has reliably applied the principles and methods to the facts of the case.[85]

The famous 1925 Scopes Monkey Trial, also known as *The State of Tennessee v. John Thomas Scopes*, was a case involving expert witnesses. In 1921 John Washington Butler sat in a Primitive Baptist Church, listening to a visiting preacher addressing the congregation. The preacher told of a young woman in his Tennessee community who enrolled in a biology course at a nearby university. When the woman finished the course and returned home, she was no longer a Christian. The theory of evolution had destroyed her faith in God. Butler, a rugged corn and tobacco farmer, listened to the preacher's sermon and began asking himself whether evolution could turn one of his own children away from God. Could this happen to his neighbors' children? He grew more worried, realizing that evolution was taught, not only in nearby universities, but in the high schools of his own Macon County.

---

[85] http://www.law.cornell.edu/rules/fre/rule_702 . The Cornell University Law Information Institute Rule 702. Testimony by Expert Witnesses.

The following year, in 1922, Butler ran as a Democrat for state representative, promising voters in his district, three counties northeast of Nashville, that he would work to protect school children from the effects of evolution. Butler won the election and, in February 1925 the Tennessee legislature enacted House Bill No. 185, known as the Butler Act, making it unlawful "to teach any theory that denies the story of divine creation as taught by the Bible and to teach instead that man was descended from a lower order of animals."[86]

In 1925 John T. Scopes was a teacher at Rhea County Central High School in Dayton, Tennessee, where he taught algebra, chemistry, and physics. At the same time, the American Civil Liberties Union (ACLU) wanted to challenge the Butler Act in court. While he was not a biology teacher, Scopes volunteered to be tried under the new law because he saw the case as a chance to stand up for academic freedom. He admitted he had used a textbook that supported evolution while serving as a substitute biology teacher. That was enough to get him charged under the new law.[87]

In July 1925 the trial began. William Jennings Bryan, a three-time presidential candidate, argued for the prosecution, while Clarence Darrow, an agnostic and famed defense attorney, represented Scopes. The case was both a theological contest as well as a trial concerning whether the theory of evolution should be taught in schools. John Butler sat in the front row. As part of his defense strategy, Darrow contended that there was actually no conflict between evolution and the creation account in the Bible. In support of this claim, Darrow brought in eight experts on evolution, although only one of these expert witnesses, Dr. Maynard Metcalf, a zoologist from Johns Hopkins University, was allowed to testify in person. The judge allowed the other experts to submit written statements.

At one point in the trial, Clarence Darrow took the uncommon step of calling William Jennings Bryan, the prosecutor in the case, to the stand as a witness in an effort to demonstrate that belief in the historicity of the Bible and its many accounts of miracles was unreasonable. Bryan accepted, on the understanding that Darrow would in turn submit to questioning by Bryan.

---

[86] PUBLIC ACTS OF THE STATE OF TENNESSEE PASSED BY THE SIXTY - FOURTH GENERAL ASSEMBLY 1925, CHAPTER NO. 27. House Bill No. 185.

[87] http://www.biography.com/people/john-scopes-17183774#evolution-on-trial&awesm=~oBCtwsDp7duLYe

On the night before Bryan's testimony, Darrow prepared by having scientists answer questions as they believed Bryan would.

Questioning Bryan the next day, Darrow began a series of queries designed to undermine a literalist interpretation of the Bible. Darrow asked Bryan about a great fish swallowing Jonah, Joshua making the sun stand still, Noah and the great flood, the temptation of Adam in the Garden, and the Genesis account of creation. After initially contending that everything in the Bible should be accepted as it is written, Bryan conceded that some information in the Bible should not be taken literally. In response to Darrow's relentless questions as to whether the six days of creation, as described in Genesis, were twenty-four hour days, Bryan said "My impression is that they were periods."[88] Bryan, who began his testimony calmly, stumbled badly under Darrow's persistent prodding. At one point the exasperated Bryan said, "I do not think about things I don't think about." Darrow asked, "Do you think about the things you do think about?"

In the end, Darrow himself asked the jury to return a guilty verdict so that the case could be appealed to a higher court. Scopes was found guilty and fined $100, but the verdict was overturned on a technicality. The case was never retried.

Expert witnesses are typically conversant in a particular field. For example, a forensic scientist may be called upon to testify regarding the credibility of certain physical evidence; a psychologist may be asked to testify to the competence of a defendant to stand trial; and a mechanical engineer could be brought in to explain how a certain machine may have broken down in a given situation. The experts called to testify in the Scopes Trial were university biology professors knowledgeable about evolution.

In a 2008 episode of CSI, the crime drama starring William Petersen as forensic scientist Gil Grissom, the Las Vegas District Attorney Maddie Klein called on Grissom and his team to investigate the deaths of several key witnesses for a grand jury case against a dangerous Las Vegas gang. The gang was terrorizing and murdering witnesses who could land them in prison. Klein also needed Grissom to be an expert witness in the Grand Jury case against the gang. Grissom was reluctant, but the DA insisted that he was the only one for the job because of his expertise in forensic science.

---

[88] http://law2.umkc.edu/faculty/projects/ftrials/scopes/evolut.htm. From *State v. John Scopes ("The Monkey Trial")*
by Douglas O. Linder.

Since Jesus' case was one concerning faith and religion, John sought out an expert in religious matters. In John 3, John called an expert witness named Nicodemus to testify concerning Jesus.

> Now there was a Pharisee, a man named Nicodemus who was a member of the Jewish ruling council. He came to Jesus at night and said, "*Rabbi, we know that you are a teacher who has come from God. For no one could perform the signs you are doing if God were not with him.*"
>
> Jesus replied, "Very truly I tell you, no one can see the kingdom of God unless they are born again."[89]

Calling Nicodemus to testify was risky due to the fact that, at the point in the story when John called him to the witness stand, Nicodemus was not a follower of Jesus; he was only a seeker. But Nicodemus was a credible expert witness for the following reasons: (1) The name Nicodemus meant "victory over the people." It was probably a well-known and respected family name that reflected Nicodemus' influence in the community. (2) Nicodemus was a Pharisee. The Pharisees controlled the synagogues and were the most well-known religious group in Jerusalem at the time of Jesus. Every mother wanted her son to grow up to be a Pharisee. These men were well-respected and credible. (3) Nicodemus was a ruler of the Jews. This meant that he was a member of the Sanhedrin, the 70-member body that was the equivalent of the United States Supreme Court.[90]

John asked Nicodemus the same question he asked his other witnesses: What do you think about Jesus? Who is he? Nicodemus answered, "*We know that Jesus is a teacher who has come from God, for no man could do the miracles he has done unless God is with him.*"[91] The fact that this statement came from someone who was not yet a follower of Jesus made it all the more extraordinary. A witness who was an expert in religion, and who was not a follower of Christ, had yet testified in favor of Christ. Of course, we know that later Nicodemus became a follower of Jesus.

John:	Please state your name for the court.
Nicodemus:	My name is Nicodemus.

---

[89] John 3:1-3
[90] John 3:1
[91] John 3:2

John:	Nicodemus, you are a member of the Pharisees, is that right?
Nicodemus:	Yes, I am.
John:	You are also a member of the Sanhedrin, is that correct?
Nicodemus:	Yes.
John:	And can you tell the jury what the Sanhedrin is?
Nicodemus:	The Sanhedrin is the Jewish Ruling Council. It is the supreme religious body as well as the highest court in all the land of Israel.
John:	Your name, 'Nicodemus,' means 'victory over the people.' Would you say that you are a man of high reputation in Palestine?
Nicodemus:	I could not say. That would be for others to judge.
John:	Very well. Is it safe to say that you are an expert when it comes to questions concerning religious faith?
Nicodemus:	I have spent my entire life studying the faith. I hold a high religious office. If that makes me an expert, then I suppose I am.
John:	Have you met the defendant, Jesus who is called the Christ?
Nicodemus:	Yes, I have met him.
John:	Is it true that you made a nighttime visit to Jesus?
Nicodemus:	I did.
John:	What was the purpose of your visit?
Nicodemus:	For some time, I have had an interest in him and his teaching. I wanted to meet him, learn more about him. Many people were following him. His

teaching intrigued me. The works he performed are quite remarkable.

John: When you visited Jesus that night, what did you discuss with him?

Nicodemus: We talked about God, about knowing God, about God's Spirit.

John: So Nicodemus, you are a man who is well-known, a man of great faith; you are a member of one of the most influential religious sects in Palestine; and you are a member of the Sanhedrin. Therefore, you certainly are qualified to draw conclusions about Jesus. Give us your expert opinion about him.

Nicodemus: We know that he is a teacher who has come from God. No one could perform the miraculous signs that he was doing if God were not with him.

John: We?

Nicodemus: Pardon?

John: You said 'we know' instead of 'I know.' Are you saying that you are not the only religious leader who believes that Jesus has come from God? That other religious leaders also recognize that Jesus has come from God?

Nicodemus: Yes.

John: Thank you. I have no more questions for this witness.

Nicodemus: That is all? I can tell you more!

John: No! No! You have said everything we need for you to say. Thank you! You may sit down.

Judge: Does the prosecution wish to cross-examine the witness?

Prosecutor Shaytan Kakos: Yes, your Honor, we do. Nicodemus, since you are a Pharisee as well as a

	member of our esteemed Sanhedrin, you are a person who prides himself in the truth, are you not?
Nicodemus:	Yes, I believe in the truth.
Prosecutor Shaytan Kakos:	Well, in your conversation with Jesus on the night you went to see him, you stated that you believed Jesus had been sent from God. Correct?
Nicodemus:	Yes, I did say that.
Prosecutor Shaytan Kakos:	But I could not help but notice that you stopped short of saying that Jesus *IS* God. Am I correct that you stopped short of saying that Jesus *IS* God?
Nicodemus:	Well, I—
Prosecutor Shaytan Kakos:	Is it or is it not true, Nicodemus, that you stopped short of saying that Jesus *is* God? Yes or no.
Nicodemus:	Yes, that is true, but—
Prosecutor Shaytan Kakos:	Nicodemus, do you believe that Adam in the Old Testament came from God?
Nicodemus:	Why yes, I do. I fail to see what Adam has to do with this, but—
Prosecutor Shaytan Kakos:	And what about Noah? Do you think Noah was sent by God?
Nicodemus:	I suppose so, yes.
Prosecutor Shaytan Kakos:	And Abraham?
Nicodemus:	Yes.
Prosecutor Shaytan Kakos:	What about Moses? Do you think Moses came from God?
John:	Objection, your Honor! Is there some point to these questions?
Prosecutor Shaytan Kakos:	Your Honor, I assure you there is a point and I will get to it.
Judge:	Objection overruled! But get to your point, counselor!

Prosecutor Shaytan Kakos:	Nicodemus, do you believe that our High Priest Caiaphas was sent from God? Surely you do!
Nicodemus:	Well, certainly I believe High Priest Caiaphas was sent from God.
Prosecutor Shaytan Kakos:	In fact, one could say that virtually every person who has ever lived is in some way sent from God, is that not correct, Nicodemus?
Nicodemus:	That is not what I meant—
Prosecutor Shaytan Kakos:	Is it not true that every person in one way or another is sent by God to this earth to fulfil some God-given purpose?
Nicodemus:	Well, yes, I do believe that.
Prosecutor Shaytan Kakos:	So, for you to say that Jesus was sent from God is nothing out of the ordinary since you also believe that every person is sent by God to some extent. I mean, I could say that I believe you or even I were sent from God. Now, does that make sense?
Nicodemus:	Well, yes, it makes sense, but—
Prosecutor Shaytan Kakos:	Now, let us assume that Jesus indeed was sent from God, just as all of us are sent from God. Does the fact that he might have been sent from God also mean that Jesus IS God?
Nicodemus:	No. Of course not!
Prosecutor Shaytan Kakos:	No, of course not. Nicodemus, did you know, surely you know, that our High Priest Caiaphas, who you admitted (and I certainly agree) was definitely sent from God, and who has much more authority than do you, does not believe that Jesus the so-called Christ was sent from God, at least not in any way that

	is different from anyone else being sent from God?
Nicodemus:	Yes, I am aware that High Priest Caiaphas does not—
Prosecutor Shaytan Kakos:	That High Priest Caiaphas does not what, Nicodemus?
Nicodemus:	That he does not think highly of the man Jesus.
Prosecutor Shaytan Kakos:	Indeed! Now, Nicodemus, it is clear that you admired Jesus. But, for the most part, you admired Jesus in a private, secretive kind of way, did you not?
Nicodemus:	Well, I—
Prosecutor Shaytan Kakos:	You were afraid to let your colleagues on the Sanhedrin know about your admiration for Jesus. Correct?
Nicodemus:	That was true, yes. But—
Prosecutor Shaytan Kakos:	My! My! I would think if you really admired Jesus as much as you say, you would have shouted it from every housetop in Jerusalem!
John:	Objection, your Honor!
Prosecutor Shaytan Kakos:	No further questions, your Honor!

7 What Two Founding Fathers Had to Say

One of the most frequently heard questions in Supreme Court decisions is "What was the original intent of America's Founding Fathers?" It seems that everyone has an opinion about what the Founders intended in a given situation. A 2013 Gallup survey revealed that most Americans believe the nation's Founding Fathers would not agree with the way the Constitution is being followed today and would be disappointed with how the country has turned out.[92] The poll showed that 71 percent of Americans think the signers of the Declaration of Independence would not be happy with modern-day America—up from 27 percent who said the Founders would not be pleased in 2001.[93] These survey results assume a certain level of understanding concerning what our forefathers would want.

How great would it be if somehow we could call George Washington or James Madison or Thomas Jefferson to the witness stand so that we could ask them exactly what they meant concerning certain issues such as church and state, or states' rights, or the right to bear arms? We could ask them why they did not apply the principles of freedom to slaves, what their original intent was on freedom of the press, and how that would apply to pornography or Edward Snowden. How would they feel about the right to life and privacy, and how would they apply these beliefs to the issues of gay marriage and abortion?

Unfortunately, we are unable to call our Founding Fathers to the stand. Even if we could call them to the stand, we cannot be sure that all of our questions would be resolved since they did not always agree with each other. For this reason, determining the original intent of the Founders is

[92] http://www.gallup.com/poll/163361/proud-american.aspx
[93] http://www.nbcnews.com/news/us-news/poll-71-percent-americans-say-founding-fathers-would-be-disappointed-v19287604

not always easy. Moreover, not everyone agrees that the modern application of laws should be dictated by the original intent of our nation's Founders. Irving Robert Kaufman, a federal judge appointed by President Harry Truman, wrote in a 1986 New York Times article:

> As a Federal judge, I have found it often difficult to ascertain the "intent of the framers," and even more problematic to try to dispose of a constitutional question by giving great weight to the intent argument. Indeed, even if it were possible to decide hard cases on the basis of a strict interpretation of original intent, or originalism, that methodology would conflict with a judge's duty to apply the Constitution's underlying principles to changing circumstances. Furthermore, by attempting to erode the base for judicial affirmation of the freedoms guaranteed by the Bill of Rights and the 14th Amendment (no state shall "deprive any person of life, liberty, or property without due process of law; nor deny to any person . . . the equal protection of the laws"), the intent theory threatens some of the greatest achievements of the Federal judiciary.[94]

It is a fact that the Founders themselves were not so big on clinging to their original intent with regard to specifics. On the floor of the Congress in 1796, Founding Father James Madison declared:

> Whatever veneration might be entertained for the body of men who formed our Constitution, sense of that body could never be regarded as the oracular guide in expounding the Constitution.[95]

With which of America's Founding Fathers would you like to have a discussion? Personally, I am most intrigued with Thomas Jefferson. I am not the only person who has been fascinated by Jefferson. At a White House dinner honoring Nobel Prize winners of the western hemisphere, President John F. Kennedy, on April 29, 1962, remarked:

> I think this is the most extraordinary collection of talent, of human knowledge, that has ever been gathered together at the

---

[94] http://www.nytimes.com/1986/02/23/magazine/what-did-the-founding-fathers-intend.html?pagewanted=1
[95] Ibid.

> White House, with the possible exception of when Thomas Jefferson dined alone.[96]

President Kennedy went on to say:

> Someone once said that Thomas Jefferson was a gentleman of 32 who could calculate an eclipse, survey an estate, tie an artery, plan an edifice, try a cause, break a horse, and dance the minuet. Whatever he may have lacked, if he could have had his former colleague, Mr. Franklin, here we all would have been impressed.[97]

In proving his case for Jesus, John called Moses and Abraham, two "Founding Fathers" from Israel's past, to testify on Jesus' behalf. In John's opinion, the original intent of these two Founders regarding Jesus was never in doubt.

John Called Moses to the Stand.

John referred to Jesus by name twelve times in John chapter 7. Next to the name Jesus, the person whose name occurred more frequently than any other in John 7 was Moses. In a sense, John was calling Moses to testify. He had already alluded to Moses once before in John 5, where Jesus said,

> If you believed Moses, you would believe me, for he wrote about me. But since you do not believe what he wrote, how are you going to believe what I say?[98]

In chapter 7, John made at least seven connections to Moses.

The first connection was the Feast of Tabernacles. (vs. 1-2)

These verses below paved the way for one of Jesus' journeys to Jerusalem in which he celebrated the Feast of Tabernacles.

---

[96] John F. Kennedy: "Remarks at a Dinner Honoring Nobel Prize Winners of the Western Hemisphere.," April 29, 1962. Online by Gerhard Peters and John T. Woolley, The American Presidency Project. http://www.presidency.ucsb.edu/ws/?pid=8623.

[97] Ibid.

[98] John 5:46-47

> After this, Jesus went around in Galilee, purposely staying away from Judea because the Jews there were waiting to take his life. But when the Jewish Feast of Tabernacles was near…[99]

The Feast of Tabernacles began on the fifteenth day of the Hebrew month of Tishrei, a date that varies from late September to late October. It is one of the three biblically mandated feasts in which Jews were encouraged to make a pilgrimage to the Temple in Jerusalem. It commemorates the Wilderness wanderings of the Israelites recorded in Exodus, Leviticus, Numbers, and Deuteronomy. The tabernacles, also called booths, were tents the Israelites lived in during the forty years that they wandered in the Wilderness. The leader of the Israelites at the time of the Wilderness wanderings was Moses. By emphasizing in chapter 7 that it was at the Feast of Tabernacles that Jesus went to Jerusalem, John connected Jesus to Moses.

The second connection was the mocking of Jesus' siblings. (vs. 3-5) There were times in the lives of both Moses and Jesus when their siblings proved disagreeable. John 7 described how Jesus' own brothers rejected him.

> Jesus' brothers said to him, "You ought to leave here and go to Judea, so that your disciples may see the miracles you do. No one who wants to become a public figure acts in secret. Since you are doing these things, show yourself to the world." For even his own brothers did not believe in him.[100]

The writer of the book of Numbers described how, in the Wilderness, Moses' siblings, Aaron and Miriam, criticized Moses because of his marriage to a Cushite woman from the land of Cush, near Ethiopia. The woman most likely was darker skinned, hinting at the possibility that Miriam and Aaron harbored some racial prejudice against the woman. Whatever their feelings about Moses' new wife, Miriam and Aaron took this opportunity to criticize Moses because they were envious of Moses' leadership.

> Miriam and Aaron began to talk against Moses because of his Cushite wife, for he had married a Cushite. "Has the LORD

---

[99] John 7:1-2

[100] John 7:3-5

> spoken only through Moses?" they asked. "Hasn't he also spoken through us?" And the LORD heard this.[101]

By highlighting the extraordinary fact that Jesus' own brothers at one point did not believe in him, John again connected Jesus to Moses who experienced the same from his brother and sister.

The third connection was the gossiping among the people. (vs. 11-13) Jesus' presence in Jerusalem often provoked questions and gossip among the people who were gathered there. In verses 11-13, John described some of the murmuring that went on during Jesus' visit to Jerusalem at the Feast of Tabernacles.

> Now at the Feast the Jews were watching for him and asking, "Where is that man?" Among the crowds there was widespread whispering about him. Some said, "He is a good man." Others replied, "No, he deceives the people." But no one would say anything publicly about him for fear of the Jews.[102]

When this murmuring about Jesus is compared to the grumbling of the Israelites against Moses in the Wilderness (Exodus 16:1-3, and Numbers 14:1-11 below), we see that John again connected Jesus to Moses through these mutual experiences.

> The whole Israelite community set out from Elim and came to the Desert of Sin, which is between Elim and Sinai, on the fifteenth day of the second month after they had come out of Egypt. In the desert the whole community grumbled against Moses and Aaron. The Israelites said to them, "If only we had died by the LORD's hand in Egypt! There we sat around pots of meat and ate all the food we wanted, but you have brought us out into this desert to starve this entire assembly to death."[103]
>
> That night all the people of the community raised their voices and wept aloud. All the Israelites grumbled against Moses and Aaron, and the whole assembly said to them, "If only we had died in Egypt! Or in this desert! Why is the LORD bringing us

[101] Numbers 12:1-3
[102] John 7:11-13
[103] Exodus 16:1-3

> to this land only to let us fall by the sword? Our wives and children will be taken as plunder. Wouldn't it be better for us to go back to Egypt?" And they said to each other, "We should choose a leader and go back to Egypt." Then Moses and Aaron fell face down in front of the whole Israelite assembly gathered there. But the whole assembly talked about stoning them. Then the glory of the LORD appeared at the Tent of Meeting to all the Israelites. The LORD said to Moses, "How long will these people treat me with contempt? How long will they refuse to believe in me, in spite of all the miraculous signs I have performed among them?"[104]

The fourth connection was Moses' giving of the Law. (vs. 16, 19, 21-23) The verses below from John 7 detail a discussion between Jesus and the Jewish religious leaders on what was allowable behavior on the Sabbath. Naturally, the conversation turned to the Jewish Law.

> Jesus answered, "My teaching is not my own. It comes from him who sent me…Has not Moses given you the law? Yet not one of you keeps the law. Why are you trying to kill me?"
>
> Jesus said to them, "I did one miracle, and you are all astonished. Yet, because Moses gave you circumcision (though actually it did not come from Moses, but from the patriarchs), you circumcise a child on the Sabbath. Now if a child can be circumcised on the Sabbath so that the law of Moses may not be broken, why are you angry with me for healing the whole man on the Sabbath?"[105]

In this discussion, Jesus highlighted Moses' giving the Law to Israel.[106] The Sabbath commandment encouraged people to rest on the seventh day of the week. By the time of Jesus, Jewish religious experts had expanded this command to prohibit all manner of even minor conduct on the Sabbath. The Law also stipulated that male children be circumcised a few days after birth.

> The LORD said to Moses, "Say to the Israelites: 'A woman who becomes pregnant and gives birth to a son will be ceremonially

[104] Numbers 14:1-5, 10-11
[105] John 7:16, 19, 21-23
[106] See Exodus 20

> unclean for seven days, just as she is unclean during her monthly period. On the eighth day the boy is to be circumcised.'"[107]

By including this debate between Jesus and the religious leaders, John again connected Jesus to Moses.

The fifth connection was Moses' going away without ever being found. (vs. 32-36)

As Jesus' argument with the crowds continued, Jesus stated that he would be on earth for a short time, and then return to God, after which time the religious leaders would not be able to find him. Jesus' comments left the leaders pondering what he meant.

> The Pharisees heard the crowd whispering such things about him. Then the chief priests and the Pharisees sent temple guards to arrest him. Jesus said, "I am with you for only a short time, and then I go to the one who sent me. You will look for me, but you will not find me; and where I am, you cannot come."
>
> The Jews said to one another, "Where does this man intend to go that we cannot find him?"[108]

In relating this discussion, John linked Jesus to Moses in that, just as when Moses died, his body was not found, even so when Jesus went away, his body, at least at first, would not be found. In fact, the religious leaders never found Jesus' body.

> Then Moses climbed Mount Nebo from the plains of Moab to the top of Pisgah, across from Jericho. There the LORD showed him the whole land—
>
> Then the LORD said to him, "This is the land I promised on oath to Abraham, Isaac and Jacob when I said, 'I will give it to your descendants.' I have let you see it with your eyes, but you will not cross over into it."
>
> And Moses the servant of the LORD died there in Moab, as the LORD had said. He buried him in Moab, in the valley opposite Beth Peor, but to this day no one knows where his grave is.

---

[107] Leviticus 12:1-3

[108] John 7:32-36

> Since then, no prophet has risen in Israel like Moses, whom the LORD knew face to face, who did all those miraculous signs and wonders the LORD sent him to do in Egypt…[109]

The sixth connection was Moses bringing water from the rock. (vs. 37-39)

On the last day of the Feast of Tabernacles, Jesus preached about living water. He said that streams of living water will flow from within every person who believes in him.

> On the last and greatest day of the Feast, Jesus stood and said in a loud voice, "If anyone is thirsty, let him come to me and drink. Whoever believes in me, as the Scripture has said, streams of living water will flow from within him." By this he meant the Spirit, whom those who believed in him were later to receive…[110]

The fact that Jesus made this statement about living water is notable because, on the last day of the Feast of Tabernacles, the Jews traditionally commemorate the time when God brought water from a rock for the Israelites to drink while they were in the Wilderness. Exodus 17 described one of two events in which God miraculously provided water to the thirsty Israelites.

> The whole Israelite community set out from the Desert of Sin, traveling from place to place as the Lord commanded. They camped at Rephidim, but there was no water for the people to drink. So they quarreled with Moses and said, "Give us water to drink."
>
> Moses replied, "Why do you quarrel with me? Why do you put the Lord to the test?"
>
> But the people were thirsty for water there, and they grumbled against Moses. They said, "Why did you bring us up out of Egypt to make us and our children and livestock die of thirst?"
>
> Then Moses cried out to the Lord, "What am I to do with these people? They are almost ready to stone me."
>
> The Lord answered Moses, "Go out in front of the people. Take with you some of the elders of Israel and take in

[109] Deuteronomy 34:1a, 4-5, 10-11

[110] John 7:37-39

> your hand the staff with which you struck the Nile, and go. I will stand there before you by the rock at Horeb. Strike the rock, and water will come out of it for the people to drink." So Moses did this in the sight of the elders of Israel.[111]

Numbers 20 recorded the second event in which God quenched the Israelites' thirst during their sojourn in the desert. This event is pivotal because in it, Moses disobeyed God's specific command. God told Moses to *speak* to the rock; but Moses *struck* the rock as he had done in the previous occurrence. As a result of this disobedience, God prohibited Moses from entering the Promised Land. The Gospels point out that Jesus, on the other hand, was fully obedient to God's commands, and thus is able to see believers into the Promised Land of Heaven.

> The LORD said to Moses…"Speak to that rock before their eyes and it will pour out its water. You will bring water out of the rock for the community so they and their livestock can drink."
>
> Then Moses raised his arm and struck the rock twice with his staff. Water gushed out, and the community and their livestock drank. But the LORD said to Moses and Aaron, "Because you did not trust in me enough to honor me as holy in the sight of the Israelites, you will not bring this community into the land I give them."[112]

The seventh connection had to do with the people calling Jesus "the Prophet," a title that fulfilled a prophecy originally made by and with reference to Moses. (v. 40)

According to Deuteronomy 18, Moses said God would raise up a prophet like Moses, and that Israel must listen to him.

> The nations you will dispossess listen to those who practice sorcery or divination. But as for you, the LORD your God has not permitted you to do so. The LORD your God will raise up for you a prophet like me from among your own brothers. You must listen to him… I will raise up for them a prophet like you from among their brothers; I will put my words in his mouth, and he will tell them everything I command him.[113]

---

[111] Exodus 17:1-6

[112] Numbers 20:7, 8b, 11-12

[113] Deuteronomy 18:14-15, 18

In John 7, John connected Jesus to this prophecy.

> On hearing his words, some of the people said, "Surely this man is the Prophet."
>
> Others said, "He is the Messiah."
>
> Still others asked, "How can the Messiah come from Galilee? Does not Scripture say that the Messiah will come from David's descendants and from Bethlehem, the town where David lived?" Thus the people were divided because of Jesus. Some wanted to seize him, but no one laid a hand on him.[114]

Of all the famous people John could bring back to life, the one who would command the most respect from the people was Moses. So John called their hero to the witness stand. And when Moses testified about Jesus, he said, "He's the One we've all been looking for." According to John, Jesus was the one Moses wrote about; Jesus was the embodiment of Moses; and Jesus is more than Moses.

John Called Abraham to the Stand.

In chapter 8, he focused on Abraham and called him to the stand.

> To the Jews who had believed him, Jesus said, "If you hold to my teaching, you are really my disciples. Then you will know the truth, and the truth will set you free."
>
> They answered him, "We are Abraham's descendants and have never been slaves of anyone. How can you say that we shall be set free?"
>
> Jesus replied, "Very truly I tell you, everyone who sins is a slave to sin. Now a slave has no permanent place in the family, but a son belongs to it forever. So if the Son sets you free, you will be free indeed. I know that you are Abraham's descendants. Yet you are looking for a way to kill me, because you have no room for my word. I am telling you what I have seen in the Father's presence, and you are doing what you have heard from your father."[115]

[114] John 7:40-44

[115] John 8:31-38

John mentioned Abraham eleven times in this chapter, and did not mention him anywhere else in his Gospel. John made three incredible declarations concerning the relationship between Jesus and Abraham.

At the time that Abraham lived, Jesus lived and Abraham obeyed Jesus. (vs. 39-41)

Abraham lived sometime around 2000 B.C. Since Jesus is the eternal God (John 1:1), he was alive at the time Abraham lived, and therefore, observed everything Abraham did. In verses 39-41, Jesus implied that, unlike the Jews who tried to kill him, Abraham never tried to kill or disobey Jesus, but rather sought to obey God.

> "Abraham is our father," they answered.
>
> "If you were Abraham's children," said Jesus, "then you would do what Abraham did. As it is, you are looking for a way to kill me, a man who has told you the truth that I heard from God. Abraham did not do such things. You are doing the works of your own father."[116]

Abraham was alive when Jesus came to earth and rejoiced to see the day of Jesus' coming. (v. 56-57)

According to these verses, Abraham anticipated the day Jesus would come. Abraham saw that day and rejoiced because of it.

> "You are not yet fifty years old," the Jews said to him, "and you have seen Abraham!"
>
> "Your father Abraham rejoiced at the thought of seeing my day; he saw it and was glad."[117]

This means that Abraham was alive at the time Jesus came. Jesus did not mean that Abraham was physically alive on earth. Rather, Abraham was able to observe the advent of Jesus from the vantage point of Heaven.

---

[116] John 8:39-41

[117] John 8:56-57

Jesus was living before Abraham was even born and is greater than Abraham. (v. 58)

Verse 58 contains one of Jesus' famous "I Am" statements, although it is not one of the more familiar "I Am" statements.

> "I tell you the truth," Jesus answered,
> "before Abraham was born, I am!"[118]

In making this statement, Jesus made two claims: first, he stated that he existed before Abraham ever lived; second, Jesus aligned himself on the same level as God since "I Am" was the name God used for himself with Moses on Mount Sinai.[119] Clearly, John wanted his readers to recognize Jesus for who he is, the eternal God.

---

[118] John 8:58

[119] See Exodus 3:14.

8 Witnesses for the Prosecution

In a courtroom, there are always two sides, the defense and the prosecution. The defense attorney is not the only lawyer who calls witnesses, presents evidence, and so forth. In John 1, the prosecution questioned John the Baptizer. In John 9, the prosecution grilled a blind man. Here, in John 18, the prosecution examined more witnesses. If you were the prosecuting attorney, what witnesses would you call to the stand? Of course, you would call witnesses whose testimonies would work *against* Jesus. You would probably call the people depicted in John 18. Some of the witnesses are surprising. All of their testimonies were damaging. The prosecution's witnesses were Judas, Caiaphas the High Priest, Simon Peter, an official who struck Jesus for being disrespectful to the High Priest, and Pilate. The following passages from John 18 highlighted these prosecution witnesses.

> When he had finished praying, Jesus left with his disciples and crossed the Kidron Valley. On the other side there was a garden, and he and his disciples went into it.[120]
>
> **Judas**
> Now Judas, who betrayed him, knew the place, because Jesus had often met there with his disciples. So Judas came to the garden, guiding a detachment of soldiers and some officials from the chief priests and the Pharisees. They were carrying torches, lanterns and weapons.
>
> Jesus, knowing all that was going to happen to him, went out and asked them, "Who is it you want?"
>
> "Jesus of Nazareth," they replied.

[120] John 18:1

"I am he," Jesus said. (And Judas the traitor was standing there with them.) When Jesus said, "I am he," they drew back and fell to the ground.

Again he asked them, "Who is it you want?"

"Jesus of Nazareth," they said.

Jesus answered, "I told you that I am he. If you are looking for me, then let these men go." This happened so that the words he had spoken would be fulfilled: "I have not lost one of those you gave me."[121]

Peter's First Denial

Simon Peter and another disciple were following Jesus. Because this disciple was known to the high priest, he went with Jesus into the high priest's courtyard, but Peter had to wait outside at the door. The other disciple, who was known to the high priest, came back, spoke to the servant girl on duty there and brought Peter in.

"You aren't one of this man's disciples too, are you?" she asked Peter.

He replied, "I am not."

It was cold, and the servants and officials stood around a fire they had made to keep warm. Peter also was standing with them, warming himself.[122]

Caiaphas High Priest Questions Jesus

Meanwhile, the high priest questioned Jesus about his disciples and his teaching.

"I have spoken openly to the world," Jesus replied. "I always taught in synagogues or at the temple, where all the Jews come together. I said nothing in secret. Why question me? Ask those who heard me. Surely they know what I said."[123]

The Servant who Struck Jesus

When Jesus said this, one of the officials nearby slapped him in the face. "Is this the way you answer the high priest?" he demanded.

---

[121] John 18:2-9

[122] John 18:15-18

[123] John 18:19-21

"If I said something wrong," Jesus replied, "testify as to what is wrong. But if I spoke the truth, why did you strike me?" Then Annas sent him bound to Caiaphas the high priest.[124]

Peter's Second and Third Denials

Meanwhile, Simon Peter was still standing there warming himself. So they asked him, "You aren't one of his disciples too, are you?"

He denied it, saying, "I am not."

One of the high priest's servants, a relative of the man whose ear Peter had cut off, challenged him, "Didn't I see you with him in the garden?" Again Peter denied it, and at that moment a rooster began to crow.[125]

Jesus Before Pilate

Then the Jewish leaders took Jesus from Caiaphas to the palace of the Roman governor. By now it was early morning, and to avoid ceremonial uncleanness they did not enter the palace, because they wanted to be able to eat the Passover. So Pilate came out to them and asked, "What charges are you bringing against this man?"

"If he were not a criminal," they replied, "we would not have handed him over to you."

Pilate said, "Take him yourselves and judge him by your own law."

"But we have no right to execute anyone," they objected. This took place to fulfill what Jesus had said about the kind of death he was going to die.

Pilate then went back inside the palace, summoned Jesus and asked him, "Are you the king of the Jews?"

"Is that your own idea," Jesus asked, "or did others talk to you about me?"

"Am I a Jew?" Pilate replied. "Your own people and chief priests handed you over to me. What is it you have done?"

Jesus said, "My kingdom is not of this world. If it were, my servants would fight to prevent my arrest by the Jewish leaders. But now my kingdom is from another place."

"You are a king, then!" said Pilate.

---

[124] John 18:22-24

[125] John 18:25-27

Jesus answered, "You say that I am a king. In fact, the reason I was born and came into the world is to testify to the truth. Everyone on the side of truth listens to me."

"What is truth?" retorted Pilate. With this he went out again to the Jews gathered there and said, "I find no basis for a charge against him. But it is your custom for me to release to you one prisoner at the time of the Passover. Do you want me to release 'the king of the Jews'?"

They shouted back, "No, not him! Give us Barabbas!" Now Barabbas had taken part in an uprising.[126]

Judas

A prosecuting attorney would certainly call Judas Iscariot to the witness stand. That Jesus personally chose Judas to be one of the twelve disciples, and that, in the end, Judas betrayed Jesus in such a major way, does not fare well for Jesus' judgment. Below is how the prosecution's questioning of Judas might have gone.

Prosecutor Shaytan Kakos:	Your Honor, the state calls to the stand Mr. Judas Iscariot. Would you please state your full name?
Judas Iscariot:	Judas Iscariot.
Prosecutor Shaytan Kakos:	Mr. Iscariot, you were one of the twelve disciples or followers of Jesus, were you not?
Judas Iscariot:	Yes, I was.
Prosecutor Shaytan Kakos:	One of only twelve. That is quite an exclusive group. For how long were you a follower of Jesus, Mr. Iscariot?
Judas Iscariot:	I would say about three years, maybe a little over three years.
Prosecutor Shaytan Kakos:	Do you recall a meeting you attended at the office of the High Priest on the evening of April 4th, in the sixteenth year of our Emperor Tiberius?
Judas Iscariot:	Uh, well, I can explain that, you see, I—

[126] John 18:28-40

Prosecutor Shaytan Kakos: Mr. Iscariot, I am not asking you to explain it. I am merely asking if you recall attending the meeting. Did you or did you not attend that meeting at the office of the High Priest on the evening of April 4th?

Judas Iscariot: Yes, sir, I did.

Prosecutor Shaytan Kakos: The meeting took place at your request, correct Mr. Iscariot?

Judas Iscariot: Yes, yes, it did.

Prosecutor Shaytan Kakos: Can you tell the court why you requested a meeting with the High Priest, Mr. Iscariot?

Judas Iscariot: I, I met with him to talk about Jesus.

Prosecutor Shaytan Kakos: Yes, you did! In fact, you met with him to talk about how you could betray Jesus, is that not right, Mr. Iscariot?

Judas Iscariot: Well, yes, I mean, no, well, it was not like that. It—

Prosecutor Shaytan Kakos: Is it true that you offered to hand over Jesus to the religious officials in exchange for money, Mr. Iscariot?

Judas Iscariot: Yes, sir, I did. But it was not out of betrayal. I did it because I felt that things needed to move along a little faster than they were. I felt that maybe I could nudge things along.

Prosecutor Shaytan Kakos: So you were not totally pleased with the pace at which Jesus was moving, were you Mr. Iscariot?

Judas Iscariot: Uh, I guess you could say that.

Prosecutor Shaytan Kakos: In fact, not only were you not pleased with the pace of the Nazarene's movement, but you were none too pleased with Jesus period, and that is the reason you accepted money in exchange for betraying Jesus! Isn't that correct, Mr. Iscariot?

Judas Iscariot: You are twisting my words. I was—

Prosecutor Shaytan Kakos: Now, Mr. Iscariot, am I really twisting your words? I can think of no other reason for your betrayal of Jesus other than that you finally came to the truth that this man is an imposter! I mean, what else could possibly prompt a man of your intellect to turn against Jesus?

Judas Iscariot: Well, I—wait a minute! You look like someone I should know, and your voice sounds strangely familiar to me. Have we met?

Prosecutor Shaytan Kakos: Oh, I seriously doubt it, Mr. Iscariot. Then again, you never know! You may have run into me when you went out to dinner at some point. No further questions, Mr. Iscariot!

Judge: Defense's witness.

John: Thank you, your Honor. Mr. Iscariot, you love money, do you not?

Judas Iscariot: Well, everybody loves money, I—

John: You realized too late, did you not Mr. Iscariot, that you betrayed innocent blood for 30 pieces of silver?

Judas Iscariot: Yes, I did.

John: Do you regret selling Jesus out?

Judas Iscariot: I do.

John: Did you ever tell Jesus how much you regretted betraying him?

Judas Iscariot: Well, before I had the chance to apologize, I, uh, you know—

John: Yes, I do know. No further questions, your Honor.

Judas' real motives for betraying Jesus remain unknown. After Jesus' death, Judas felt remorse for his betrayal and tried to retract his steps, but it was too late. Matthew's Gospel says that Judas took the money he received for his treachery, returned it to the priests, and then committed suicide by hanging himself.[127] In Acts 1:18, Luke says that "with the payment he received for his wickedness, Judas bought a field; there he fell headlong, his body burst open and all his intestines spilled out."[128]

High Priest Caiaphas

Caiaphas, the High Priest with whom Judas made his deal, would be a valuable witness for the prosecution. Because Caiaphas was the High Priest and thus an expert theologian, he would be a good counter witness to Nicodemus' expert testimony on behalf of Jesus. Caiaphas' testimony might look like the following.

Prosecutor Shaytan Kakos:	For the record, would you please state your name, sir?
High Priest Caiaphas:	Yes, my name is Yosef ben Caiaphas, High Priest in Jerusalem.
Prosecutor Shaytan Kakos:	High Priest Caiaphas, thank you for agreeing to testify today. Could you please tell us how long you have served as High Priest?
High Priest Caiaphas:	I was appointed by the Roman Procurator Valerus in the fourth year of Tiberius. I have been the High Priest ever since.
Prosecutor Shaytan Kakos:	Are you acquainted with a man by the name of Judas Iscariot?
High Priest Caiaphas:	Yes, I am. I met Mr. Iscariot in early April of the sixteenth year of Tiberius. He came to my office and asked to meet with me.
Prosecutor Shaytan Kakos:	And what was the purpose of that meeting, sir?

[127] Matthew 27:3-5
[128] Acts 1:18

High Priest Caiaphas:	Mr. Iscariot proposed a plan to hand over Jesus of Nazareth to us.
Prosecutor Shaytan Kakos:	Did this come as a surprise in light of the fact that Mr. Iscariot was a longtime friend of this Jesus?
High Priest Caiaphas:	Yes, we were surprised, but pleasantly so. We had been looking for a way to put a stop to Jesus of Nazareth. When Mr. Iscariot came, we took it as an opportunity sent from God. This Jesus had to be stopped and soon!
Prosecutor Shaytan Kakos:	So may I take that to mean that you do not think God had anything at all to do with sending Jesus?
High Priest Caiaphas:	Oh, goodness, no! Not in the least! If I believed there was such a thing as the devil, then perhaps the devil himself may have sent Jesus, or, for that matter, Jesus could be the devil, but certainly not God! God had nothing to do with sending Jesus!
Prosecutor Shaytan Kakos:	*If* you believed in the devil? So you do not believe in the devil?
High Priest Caiaphas:	No, I do not. No Sadducee believes in the devil or demons.
Prosecutor Shaytan Kakos:	If only more people were like you, High Priest Caiaphas!
High Priest Caiaphas:	What do you mean?
Prosecutor Shaytan Kakos:	Never mind! I was simply complimenting you on your discernment! Um, did Mr. Iscariot indicate why he was willing to make a deal to turn Jesus in?
High Priest Caiaphas:	I believe he said he had become impatient with Jesus of Nazareth, that Jesus was not headed in the right direction. I took that to mean that

	maybe Mr. Iscariot had come to his senses about Jesus.
Prosecutor Shaytan Kakos:	Come to his senses about Jesus?
High Priest Caiaphas:	Yes, he had come to realize Jesus was an imposter.
Prosecutor Shaytan Kakos:	Thank you, Mr. High Priest.
Judge:	Defense's witness.
John:	Yes, your Honor. High Priest Caiaphas, if I recall, at one point, you made the statement that it would be advantageous for one man to die on behalf of the nation, or something to that effect. Do you recall saying that?
High Priest Caiaphas:	I have always believed it would be good if one man died for the people as opposed to having the whole nation perish.
John:	So you did make this statement?
High Priest Caiaphas:	I made the statement, yes.
John:	This is an important statement because dying for the people is exactly what Jesus did!
High Priest Caiaphas:	Well, I—
John:	Mr. High Priest, do you think a man of your standing should be secretly handing money out to a liar bent on betraying his best friend?
High Priest Caiaphas:	Excuse me?
John:	I said do you think a man of your stature should be secretly handing money over to a liar who betrays his best friend?
High Priest Caiaphas:	I beg your pardon, sir, I—
John:	No further questions, your Honor.

The People Who Talked with Simon Peter on the Night of Jesus' Trial

The prosecution might call to the stand some of the people who confronted Peter on the eve of Jesus' crucifixion about whether he knew Jesus. They would testify that they saw Peter, asked him if he was a follower of Jesus, and that Peter swore to them he did not know Jesus. In light of the fact that Peter was the spokesman of the twelve disciples, and that Jesus personally selected each of his disciples, Peter's denials cast Jesus' discernment in an unfavorable light.

Asst. Prosecutor Paula Ponera:	What is your occupation?
Servant Girl:	I am a servant girl assigned to watch the trial room door when prisoners are being interrogated and flogged.
Asst. Prosecutor Paula Ponera:	Were you on duty the night Jesus the Christ was interrogated?
Servant Girl:	Yes, ma'am, I was.
Asst. Prosecutor Paula Ponera:	Do you remember seeing any of Jesus' followers that night?
Servant Girl:	I remember seeing two of Jesus' followers that night. One went into the interrogation area, and then just seconds later he came back out. He asked me if it would be okay for the second man to go in. And I said yes.
Asst. Prosecutor Paula Ponera:	Did you have any other conversations with either of these two followers of Jesus you saw that night?
Servant Girl:	Yes, ma'am. As the second man started through the trial room entrance, I thought I recognized him as one of Jesus' followers. I said to him, "You aren't one of this man's disciples too, are you?" But he replied that he was not one of Jesus' followers. I could tell he was annoyed by my question.
Asst. Prosecutor Paula Ponera:	Did anyone else hear your conversation with this man?

Servant Girl: Oh, yes, ma'am, a large crowd was gathered at the entrance. I'm sure others heard our conversation. In fact, I was not the only one who thought they recognized this man as being one of Jesus' followers. Others asked him the same question I had asked him.

Asst. Prosecutor Paula Ponera: Really! And how did the man respond to them?

Servant Girl: The same way he responded to me. He said he did not know Jesus and was not one of Jesus' followers.

Asst. Prosecutor Paula Ponera: So was he a disciple of Jesus?

Servant Girl: I thought he was, but he said he wasn't; so I guess he was not one of Jesus' disciples. I do not know who he was.

Asst. Prosecutor Paula Ponera: What would you say if I told you that the man you are referring to was not only one of Jesus' followers, but the leader of his followers?

Servant Girl: Wow! I would be surprised!

Asst. Prosecutor Paula Ponera: Well, it is true! The man who told you he was not one of Jesus' followers is actually Simon Barjonas, the ringleader of the group of twelve. The Nazarene even gave this man the nickname "Peter." This is the same man who denied being a follower of Jesus when you asked him about it. Now, based upon what this man said to you at the trial room entrance, what would you say about Jesus' impact on this man? Would you say Jesus had made much of an impact on his life?

Servant Girl: Well, I would have to say no.

Asst. Prosecutor Paula Ponera: Well, let me ask you this: considering the fact that Jesus' own right hand man

	would not even claim him after more than three years of following Jesus, why should you and I claim Jesus now?
Servant Girl:	I would say we should not.
Asst. Prosecutor Paula Ponera:	Precisely! Thank you. No further questions for this witness.

In addition to the servant girl, the prosecution called to the stand a servant of the High Priest. This man, John tells us, was a relative of the man whose ear Peter had cut off when soldiers came to arrest Jesus in Gethsemane. His brief testimony is envisioned here.

Asst. Prosecutor Ray Scotia:	Sir, you are one of the servants of the High Priest, is that right?
High Priest's Servant:	Yes, I am.
Asst. Prosecutor Ray Scotia:	Not just anyone is chosen to serve the High Priest. You must be a loyal and trustworthy man.
High Priest's Servant:	I try to be, sir.
Asst. Prosecutor Ray Scotia:	Is it true that you were among those near the entrance of the trial room on the night Jesus was interrogated?
High Priest's Servant:	Yes, sir, I was.
Asst. Prosecutor Ray Scotia:	Did you see any of Jesus' followers at any point during the trial?
High Priest's Servant:	I only saw one.
Asst. Prosecutor Ray Scotia:	Only one? Do you find that odd? I mean, what does that tell you about the impact this Jesus of Nazareth made on his own followers?
High Priest's Servant:	What do you mean?
Asst. Prosecutor Ray Scotia:	Well, Jesus had more followers than just one. So, if all but one of these followers forsook Jesus at the time he needed them most, then would you not agree that it seems that Jesus made little impact on them?

High Priest's Servant:	Well, I'd have to agree that he did not make enough of an impact for them to stay with him, if that's what you mean.
Asst. Prosecutor Ray Scotia:	Precisely! The one disciple you did see, did you talk to him?
High Priest's Servant:	I did. I am pretty sure I recognized him from when we went up to Gethsemane to arrest Jesus. He was the one who took a knife and assaulted my cousin, Malchus, cutting off Malchus' ear. When I saw the man at the interrogation entrance, I went right up to him and asked him, "Didn't I see you with Jesus in the garden?" I knew he was the one, but he denied it.
Asst. Prosecutor Ray Scotia:	You may not be aware of this, but the man of whom you are speaking was the leader of Jesus' followers. Did you know that?
High Priest's Servant:	No, sir, I did not.
Asst. Prosecutor Ray Scotia:	What do you think about the leader of Jesus' disciples denying that he was even with Jesus of Nazareth?
High Priest's Servant:	Sounds like Jesus needed to be more careful about choosing his friends!
Asst. Prosecutor Ray Scotia:	So you do not think Jesus did a good job in choosing his followers?
High Priest's Servant:	Doesn't sound like it to me.
Asst. Prosecutor Ray Scotia:	Do you not think a man truly sent from God would have used better judgment in choosing his followers?
High Priest's Servant:	Absolutely!
Asst. Prosecutor Ray Scotia:	Thank you, sir! Nothing further.

The Official Who Struck Jesus for Being Disrespectful to the Chief Priest
The prosecuting attorney might want to call the official assistant of the High Priest. This assistant was the one who slapped Jesus because he felt that Jesus had shown disrespect to the High Priest when the High Priest interrogated Jesus.

Asst. Prosecutor Ray Scotia:	State your name and occupation for the court, please.
The Official:	I am Salome ben Sirach. I am the assistant to the High Priest Caiaphas and his father-in-law Annas.
Asst. Prosecutor Ray Scotia:	Mr. Sirach, is it true that you were present on April 7th, the sixteenth year of our Emperor Tiberius, when Jesus of Nazareth was brought in for questioning by the High Priest?
The Official:	Yes, sir, I was present.
Asst. Prosecutor Ray Scotia:	Is it true that, at one point when Jesus was being questioned, you struck the defendant in the face?
The Official:	Yes, sir, I did.
Asst. Prosecutor Ray Scotia:	Can you tell the court why you struck Jesus in the face?
The Official:	Yes, sir. Annas, the father-in-law of Caiaphas, was questioning Jesus about his teaching and his followers. Annas is the most respected priest in all of Judea. Jesus spouted off some retort that was no answer at all, and then smart-mouthed High Priest Annas by questioning the High Priest's right to interrogate him. It was at that point that I struck Jesus in his face. No one humiliates the High Priest like that!
Asst. Prosecutor Ray Scotia:	So Jesus was being openly defiant and disrespectful of the high priest, is that your testimony, Mr. Sirach?

The Official:	Yes, it is. To me, that proved that this man was not from God because a man who is really from God ought to know to show respect to an elder who obviously came from God.
Asst. Prosecutor Ray Scotia:	In your opinion, does Jesus' behavior in the interrogation room fit the profile of a "God-man," Mr. Sirach?
The Official:	Not in my opinion, no, sir!
Asst. Prosecutor Ray Scotia:	Thank you, Mr. Sirach.
Judge:	Defense's witness?
John:	Mr. Sirach, if Moses had been the one to spout off at Caiaphas, as you say, would he have been wrong?
The Official:	What kind of question is that? I—
John:	Just answer the question, Mr. Sirach, would Moses have been out of line to reprimand Caiaphas?
The Official:	Sir, Moses would never have done such a thing.
John:	But if Moses were living on earth today and had done such a thing, he would not have been out of line because Moses is higher than Caiaphas, correct?
The Official:	Well, I suppose so.
John:	So, if Jesus is God as he and many others claim, then he would be even higher than Moses, and therefore, he would not have been out of line to rebuke Caiaphas either, now would he, Mr. Sirach?
The Official:	Well, I—
John:	No further questions, Mr. Sirach. You may step down.

Pontius Pilate

Any wise prosecutor would certainly call the Roman Procurator Pontius Pilate to the witness stand.

Pilate:	My name is Pontius Pilate, governor of the Roman province of Judea. I began serving as governor in the twelfth year of the reign of the Emperor Tiberius.
Prosecutor Shaytan Kakos:	Governor Pilate, thank you for agreeing to testify today. You certainly did not have to come. We appreciate you giving us some of your valuable time. I must say that it is my high honor to stand before you on this day.
Pilate:	Well, thank you.
Prosecutor Shaytan Kakos:	You questioned Jesus of Nazareth during the early morning of Passover, the day he was crucified, is that right?
Pilate:	Yes, I interrogated him.
Prosecutor Shaytan Kakos:	And you actually found no basis to the accusations being made against him by some of the Jewish people, is that right?
Pilate:	Yes, it is.
Prosecutor Shaytan Kakos:	Did you find no fault in him because of what he said, or is it that you could not actually get Jesus to answer the allegations made against him?
Pilate:	He never answered my interrogations with clear answers.
Prosecutor Shaytan Kakos:	Do you not think a man like Jesus owes the governor of Judea more respect than to dismissively avoid answering your questions?
Pilate:	I would think so, yes.
Prosecutor Shaytan Kakos:	Is that why you ultimately gave in to having Jesus crucified?
Pilate:	Well, I left that up to the crowds.

Prosecutor Shaytan Kakos: But Jesus left you little choice, did he not? I mean, if Jesus had answered your questions as he should have, you would have been less willing to turn him over to the crowds, is that not correct?

Pilate: Possibly, yes. He should have answered my questions.

Prosecutor Shaytan Kakos: Indeed he should have! Did the fact that an overwhelming majority of the people in the square believed Jesus to be worthy of death have any impact on your decision?

Pilate: Well, clearly they knew something about Jesus that I did not know. I could not ignore that. Can that many people really be wrong about this man?

Prosecutor Shaytan Kakos: Of course, they were not wrong! No further questions, your Honor.

Judge: At this time, the defense may cross-examine the witness.

John: Governor, you admitted that you interrogated Jesus on at least a couple of occasions, is that correct?

Pilate: Yes, I did.

John: And would you please share with the court your official findings concerning Jesus after you had concluded all of your interrogations?

Pilate: Well, I do not have the records in front of me, and I do not have them memorized. So I—

John: But surely you remember what you cried out to the people following those interrogations! Tell us what you told the crowds gathered that day.

Pilate:	I said, "You people take him and crucify him. As for me, I find no basis for a charge against him."
John:	"I find no basis for a charge against him," so you said. Thank you, Governor. No further questions.

Jesus' Own Brothers

The Gospel of Mark stated that Jesus had four brothers and at least two sisters. In Mark 6, Mark listed the names of the four brothers: James, Joseph, Judas, and Simon.

> Jesus left there and went to his hometown, accompanied by his disciples. When the Sabbath came, he began to teach in the synagogue, and many who heard him were amazed. "Where did this man get these things?" they asked. "What's this wisdom that has been given him? What are these remarkable miracles he is performing? Isn't this the carpenter? Isn't this Mary's son and the brother of James, Joseph, Judas and Simon? Aren't his sisters here with us?" And they took offense at him.[129]

Before Jesus' resurrection, the relationship between him and his siblings was tenuous at best. In Mark 3:21, Mark revealed that Jesus' family thought he had lost his mind, and verses 31-35 implied that, in response, Jesus may not have thought all that highly of his siblings.

> Then Jesus entered a house, and again a crowd gathered, so that he and his disciples were not even able to eat. When his family heard about this, they went to take charge of him, for they said, "He is out of his mind."[130]

> Then Jesus' mother and brothers arrived. Standing outside, they sent someone in to call him. A crowd was sitting around him, and they told him, "Your mother and brothers are outside looking for you."
>
> "Who are my mother and my brothers?" he asked.

129 Mark 6:1-3

130 Mark 3:20-21

> Then he looked at those seated in a circle around him and said, "Here are my mother and my brothers! Whoever does God's will is my brother and sister and mother."[131]

In John's Gospel, Jesus' brothers tried to coax Jesus into being more open with his ministry. Their motivation was perhaps either to get Jesus to come to his senses or to hasten his demise by convincing him to travel to Jerusalem where the Jewish leaders were out to kill him. Whatever the case, John chapter 7 revealed that Jesus' brothers did not believe in him.

> After this, Jesus went around in Galilee. He did not want to go about in Judea because the Jewish leaders there were looking for a way to kill him. But when the Jewish Festival of Tabernacles was near, Jesus' brothers said to him, "Leave Galilee and go to Judea, so that your disciples there may see the works you do. No one who wants to become a public figure acts in secret. Since you are doing these things, show yourself to the world." For even his own brothers did not believe in him.[132]

Jesus' brothers and sisters would be valuable witnesses for the prosecution if they could be convinced to testify. After all, if Jesus could not convince his own family to believe in him, why should anyone else believe in him?

Prosecutor Shaytan Kakos:	Your name, please?
Joseph, Jesus' Brother:	My name is Joseph, son of Joseph.
Prosecutor Shaytan Kakos:	How do you know Jesus of Nazareth?
Joseph, Jesus' Brother:	He is my brother.
Prosecutor Shaytan Kakos:	Your biological brother?
Joseph, Jesus' Brother:	Yes.
Prosecutor Shaytan Kakos:	Do you have other siblings?
Joseph, Jesus' Brother:	I do. In addition to Jesus, I have three other brothers, and I also have sisters.
Prosecutor Shaytan Kakos:	That's quite a large family! I'm assuming that, since you are family, you

131 Mark 3:31-35
132 John 7:1-5

	have always been a devoted follower of your brother Jesus. Is this correct?
Joseph, Jesus' Brother:	Actually, no, I am not a follower of Jesus. Never have been.
Prosecutor Shaytan Kakos:	So you are not a follower of Jesus?
Joseph, Jesus' Brother:	No. I love my brother, but, well, we thought he was losing his mind.
Prosecutor Shaytan Kakos:	We?
Joseph, Jesus' Brother:	My brothers, James, Judas, and Simon, and I. We thought Jesus had gone mad.
Prosecutor Shaytan Kakos:	Why did you think he had gone mad?
Joseph, Jesus' Brother:	Well, nothing he did made any sense to us, certainly not to me. If my brother was who he and others said he was, why was he not more vocal and visible about it? Why keep it to himself and to a select few? I know that if I could heal people or raise the dead, I would be traveling to every hospital and stopping at every cemetery to heal people and raise the dead. Instead, my brother, well, he didn't do any of those things. And what he was willing to do, he did mostly in private.
Prosecutor Shaytan Kakos:	So, what you are saying is that, though you love your brother, nothing you saw him do was congruent with what you would expect from a person with God-given healing powers, is that right?
Joseph, Jesus' Brother:	Yes, sir, sad to say it, but that is right.
Prosecutor Shaytan Kakos:	And this was not just your opinion, but the opinion of all your other brothers, including James, Judas, and Simon, is that correct?
Joseph, Jesus' Brother:	Yes, sir, that is correct.

Prosecutor Shaytan Kakos:	Now, Joseph, if Jesus' own family did not believe in him, then why should anyone else believe in him?
Joseph, Jesus' Brother:	That's a question I cannot answer.
Prosecutor Shaytan Kakos:	I can understand that. I really can. I will tell you that if you, Jesus' own brother, did not believe in Jesus, then I certainly cannot! No further questions. Thank you, sir!
Judge:	Does the defense wish to question this witness?
John:	Yes, your Honor. *(Turning his attention to the witness)* Joseph, you said your brothers did not believe in Jesus. Have you spoken with any of your brothers recently?
Joseph, Jesus' Brother:	I have had some conversations with them, yes.
John:	How about with your brother James? Have you had any conversations with him within the last few months?
Joseph, Jesus' Brother:	I have spoken briefly to him.
John:	Are you aware that your brother James, as well as some of your other siblings, came to believe in Jesus?
Joseph, Jesus' Brother:	I am aware of that, yes.
John:	And do you know what it was that prompted their change of heart regarding Jesus?
Joseph, Jesus' Brother:	They saw him after he had supposedly risen from the dead.
John:	Yes, they did! No further questions.

The Book of Acts mentioned Jesus' brothers being present at a prayer meeting in Jerusalem just after Jesus had ascended to heaven. In Acts 1:14, we read the following:

> They all joined together constantly in prayer, along with the women and Mary the mother of Jesus, and with his brothers.[133]

The text did not include the brothers' names, so we cannot know with certainty whether all of Jesus' brothers came to believe in him or if only some of them did. In Galatians 1:18-19, the Apostle Paul described how he met with James, the Lord's brother in Jerusalem. This James is believed to have been the pastor of the Jerusalem Church at the time of the first church council there in Acts 15.

---

[133] Acts 1:14

9 Relying on Historical Precedent

At times, attorneys will refer to previous court decisions in order to convince a judge or a jury of a certain opinion. This is known as relying on historical precedent. One American court case that is often relied upon for historical precedent regarding free speech cases is the landmark 1964 case, the *New York Times Co. v. Sullivan*. In 1960, as the Civil Rights Movement in the United States was gaining strength, civil rights leaders ran a full-page ad in the *New York Times* that openly criticized the police department of Montgomery, Alabama for what the ad called "an unprecedented wave of terror" against peaceful demonstrators.

The ad, titled "Heed Their Rising Voices," highlighted crimes and harassment perpetrated by, or with support or tacit approval of, some government officials against blacks and civil rights leaders in the segregated south. The full-page ad was sponsored by a group of religious and Hollywood leaders intent on exposing the abuses and driving the public debate on civil rights. The ad also sought to raise funds for Martin Luther King's legal defense fund.[134]

While most of the information in the ad was accurate, some of the charges were not true. For example, the ad said that police "ringed" a college campus where protestors were, but this charge was exaggerated. The ad also contained the false statement: "When the entire student body protested to state authorities by refusing to re-register, their dining hall was padlocked in an attempt to starve them into submission."[135]

[134] http://www.forbes.com/sites/realspin/2014/03/05/the-landmark-libel-case-times-v-sullivan-still-resonates-50-years-later/

[135] http://billofrightsinstitute.org/resources/educator-resources/lessons-plans/landmark-cases-and-the-constitution/new-york-times-v-sullivan-1964/

L.B. Sullivan, the Montgomery police commissioner, sued the *New York Times* for printing something they knew was false and would cause harm. Although the ad did not mention his name, Sullivan claimed that it implied his responsibility for the actions of the police. He said that the ad damaged his reputation in the community. The Alabama court ruled in favor of Sullivan, finding that the newspaper ad falsely represented the police department and Sullivan. The court ordered the *New York Times* to pay $500,000 in damages.

After losing an appeal in the Supreme Court of Alabama, the *New York Times* took its case to the United States Supreme Court arguing that the ad was not meant to hurt Sullivan's reputation and was protected under the First Amendment to the United States Constitution. The newspaper contended that it had no reason to believe that the advertisement included false statements, so it did not check their accuracy. Furthermore, the *Times* argued that if a newspaper had to check the accuracy of every criticism of every public official, a free press would severely be limited.

In March 1964, the United States Supreme Court unanimously ruled in favor of the newspaper, holding that the right to publish all statements is protected under the First Amendment. The Court also held that, in order to prove libel, a public official must show that what was said against them was made with actual malice – "that is, with knowledge that it was false or with reckless disregard for the truth."[136] The Court asserted America's "profound national commitment to the principle that debate on public issues should be uninhibited, robust, and wide-open." Free and open debate about the conduct of public officials, the justices reasoned, was more important than occasional, honest factual errors that might hurt or damage officials' reputations.[137]

In the decades since *New York Times v. Sullivan*, the justices have extended the decision, making it tough for celebrities, politicians, and other public figures to win libel suits. In a March 2014 *Forbes Magazine* article about the *New York Times* case, Roy S. Gutterman, an associate professor of communications law and journalism at Syracuse University, said:

---

[136]http://www.uscourts.gov/multimedia/podcasts/Landmarks/NewYorkTimesv Sullivan.aspx

[137] http://billofrightsinstitute.org/resources/educator-resources/lessons-plans/landmark-cases-and-the-constitution/new-york-times-v-sullivan-1964/

> As we approach its 50th anniversary, there may be no modern Supreme Court decision that has had more of an impact on American free speech values than the landmark New York Times Co. v. Sullivan case.[138]

Gutterman went on to say:

> In First Amendment circles, Times v. Sullivan is widely considered the most important decision the Supreme Court rendered in the modern 20th Century and one of a handful of First Amendment decisions vital to ensuring a free press and protecting free speech. Times v. Sullivan has had an impact on just about every free speech and free press case for the past half-century, influencing everything from how we accept debate and tolerate speech we disagree with to our legal definitions of privacy, obscenity and indecency. The case has been integral to forging rules for access to public meetings, public places and commercial speech as well as the free speech rights of just about anyone you care to list – journalists, confidential sources, lawyers, campaign donors, pornographers, comedians, religious zealots and hate-mongers.[139]

In January 2014, a California jury decided that singer Courtney Love should not have to pay $8 million over a troublesome statement she had made on Twitter about her former lawyer. The singer tweeted that her former lawyer, Rhonda Holmes, had been "bought off" in a suit involving the estate of Love's late husband, musician Kurt Cobain. Holmes sued Love for $8 million, claiming the tweet was false and had hurt her reputation. In winning her case, Love became just the latest person to lean on the historical precedent set by the *New York Times v. Sullivan* case as well as the cases that followed and expanded the Sullivan case. Once the Sullivan ruling came into play, the jury found that though Love published a false statement, she did not know it was false.[140]

---

[138] http://www.forbes.com/sites/realspin/2014/03/05/the-landmark-libel-case-times-v-sullivan-still-resonates-50-years-later/

[139] http://www.forbes.com/sites/realspin/2014/03/05/the-landmark-libel-case-times-v-sullivan-still-resonates-50-years-later/

[140] Jessica Gresko, *At 50, Landmark Libel Case Relevant In Digital Age*, The Associated Press, March 8, 2014. http://bigstory.ap.org/article/50-landmark-libel-case-relevant-digital-age

In his Gospel, John utilized historical precedent by looking back to the Old Testament for evidence pointing to who Jesus was. John's argument went like this:

1. Old Testament writers predicted that certain things would be true about the Messiah.
2. What the Old Testament writers predicted about the Messiah was fulfilled in Jesus.
3. Therefore, Jesus must be the Messiah.

General Old Testament Prophecies Fulfilled

There are four times in his Gospel where John referred to Jesus fulfilling *general* Old Testament predictions without actually revealing which Old Testament texts John had in mind.

The first time John referred to Jesus fulfilling Old Testament predictions was in John chapter 2.

> Jesus answered them, "Destroy this temple, and I will raise it again in three days." The Jews replied, "It has taken forty-six years to build this temple, and you are going to raise it in three days?" But the temple he had spoken of was his body. After he was raised from the dead, his disciples recalled what he had said. Then *they believed the Scripture and the words that Jesus had spoken.*[141]

The second time John referred to Jesus fulfilling general Old Testament prophecies came in John chapter 5.

> You diligently study the Scriptures because you think that by them you possess eternal life. *These are the Scriptures that testify about me,* yet you refuse to come to me to have life.[142]

In John 7:37-38, John again showed Jesus fulfilling Old Testament predictions in general.

> On the last and greatest day of the Feast, Jesus stood and said in a loud voice, "If anyone is thirsty, let him come to me and drink.

---

[141] John 2:19-22
[142] John 5:39-40

> Whoever believes in me, *as the Scripture has said*, streams of living water will flow from within him."[143]

In John chapter 20, John made a final note regarding the fact that Jesus fulfilled Old Testament expectations in general.

> So Peter and the other disciple started for the tomb. Both were running, but the other disciple outran Peter and reached the tomb first. He bent over and looked in at the strips of linen lying there but did not go in. Then Simon Peter, who was behind him, arrived and went into the tomb. He saw the strips of linen lying there, as well as the burial cloth that had been around Jesus' head. The cloth was folded up by itself, separate from the linen. Finally the other disciple, who had reached the tomb first, also went inside. He saw and believed. *(They still did not understand from Scripture that Jesus had to rise from the dead.)*[144]

Specific Old Testament Prophecies Fulfilled

In addition to the aforementioned general prophecies in John, there are eight times that John showed Jesus fulfilling *specific* Old Testament predictions. In these passages, John gave enough information to allow us to determine exactly which Old Testament text Jesus fulfilled.

The Old Testament predicted that the Messiah would come from Bethlehem.

In John 7, a discussion arose among the people concerning who Jesus was. In verses 41-42, John quoted some people asking a question in which they mentioned that the Messiah would come from Bethlehem.

> Others said, "He is the Christ." Still others asked, "How can the Christ come from Galilee? *Does not the Scripture say* that the Christ will come from David's family and from Bethlehem, the town where David lived?"[145]

While the actual Old Testament citations were not given, it is clear that the people were referring to Micah chapter 5, where Micah, an Old

---

[143] John 7:37-38
[144] John 20:3-9
[145] John 7:41-42

Testament prophet who lived during the 700s B.C.E., predicted that the Messiah would hail from Bethlehem.

> But you, Bethlehem Ephrathah, though you are small among the clans of Judah, out of you will come for me one who will be ruler over Israel, whose origins are from of old, from ancient times.[146]

The Old Testament prophesied that people would reject Jesus. Throughout John's Gospel, some people wholeheartedly believed in Jesus, while others stubbornly refused to believe in him in spite of overwhelming evidence. In John 12, John described people witnessing Jesus' miracles, and yet refusing to believe in him.

> Even after Jesus had done all these miraculous signs in their presence, they still would not believe in him. *This was to fulfill the word of Isaiah the prophet:* "Lord, who has believed our message and to whom has the arm of the Lord been revealed?" For this reason they could not believe, because, *as Isaiah says elsewhere:* "He has blinded their eyes and deadened their hearts, so they can neither see with their eyes, nor understand with their hearts, nor turn—and I would heal them." Isaiah said this because he saw Jesus' glory and spoke about him.[147]

John tied these events of unbelief to the Old Testament prophecy of Isaiah. In the passage above, John referenced two passages in the book of Isaiah, with the first reference coming from Isaiah 53, and the second reference coming from Isaiah chapter 6.

> Who has believed our message and to whom has the arm of the LORD been revealed?[148]

> Make the heart of this people calloused; make their ears dull and close their eyes. Otherwise they might see with their eyes, hear with their ears, understand with their hearts, and turn and be healed.[149]

---

146 Micah 5:2

147 John 12:37-41

148 Isaiah 53:1

149 Isaiah 6:10

In John 15, Jesus reflected on the fact that certain people hated him. Then John noted that the people's hatred of Jesus fulfilled prophecy written in the Psalms.

> If I had not done among them what no one else did, they would not be guilty of sin. But now they have seen these miracles, and yet they have hated both me and my Father. But *this is to fulfill what is written in their Law:* "They hated me without reason."[150]

The quote that "They hated me without reason" came from Psalm 35:19 and Psalm 69:4.

> Let not those gloat over me who are my enemies without cause; *let not those who hate me without reason maliciously wink the eye.*[151]

> *Those who hate me without reason* outnumber the hairs of my head; many are my enemies without cause, those who seek to destroy me. I am forced to restore what I did not steal.[152]

The Old Testament anticipated the betrayal of Jesus by Judas. In John 13:18, Jesus quoted Psalm 41 as being a prophecy concerning Judas' betrayal of Jesus into the hands of the Jewish religious leaders and the Roman authorities. Below are Jesus' words in the Gospel of John followed by the Psalm from which the words were taken.

> "I am not referring to all of you; I know those I have chosen. But *this is to fulfill the scripture:* 'He who shares my bread has lifted up his heel against me.'"[153]

> Even my close friend, whom I trusted, *he who shared my bread, has lifted up his heel against me.*[154]

---

[150] John 15:25
[151] Psalm 35:19
[152] Psalm 69:4
[153] John 13:18
[154] Psalm 41:9

In John 17, Jesus prayed for his disciples. He prayed that God would protect them after he was no longer in the world. In his prayer, Jesus again stated that the Old Testament scriptures foretold that one of the disciples was doomed to destruction. This reference to the Old Testament scripture (italics below) was again a reference to Psalm 41:9 above.

> I will remain in the world no longer, but they are still in the world, and I am coming to you. Holy Father, protect them by the power of your name, the name you gave me, so that they may be one as we are one. While I was with them, I protected them and kept them safe by that name you gave me. None has been lost except the one doomed to destruction *so that Scripture would be fulfilled.* I am coming to you now, but I say these things while I am still in the world, so that they may have the full measure of my joy within them.[155]

The Old Testament predicted that certain events would occur at Jesus' crucifixion.

In John 19, John described how, at Jesus' crucifixion, soldiers gambled for Jesus' garments.

> When the soldiers crucified Jesus, they took his clothes, dividing them into four shares, one for each of them, with the undergarment remaining. This garment was seamless, woven in one piece from top to bottom. "Let's not tear it," they said to one another. "Let's decide by lot who will get it." *This happened that the scripture might be fulfilled* which said, "They divided my garments among them and cast lots for my clothing." So this is what the soldiers did.[156]

In this text, John connected the soldiers' gambling over Jesus' clothes to Old Testament prophecy found in Psalm 22.

> They divide my garments among them
> and cast lots for my clothing.[157]

[155] John 17:11-13
[156] John 19:23-24
[157] Psalm 22:18

John 19 described how some of the people present at the crucifixion soaked a sponge in vinegar and lifted it to Jesus' mouth. John noted that this act was done to fulfill Old Testament scripture.

> Later, knowing that all was now completed, and *so that the Scripture would be fulfilled*, Jesus said, "I am thirsty." A jar of wine vinegar was there, so they soaked a sponge in it, put the sponge on a stalk of the hyssop plant, and lifted it to Jesus' lips.[158]

The Old Testament text John referred to was Psalm 69:21, in which the Psalmist said, "They put gall in my food and gave me vinegar for my thirst."

In John 19, the Roman soldiers proceeded to break the legs of the prisoners who were being crucified. This was done each time crucifixions were held on Friday because the Jewish Sabbath began each Friday at 6:00 p.m. The Jews held that it was unlawful for bodies to be taken down from crosses and entombed on the Sabbath. The Roman authorities, ever sensitive to Jewish beliefs, broke the bones of those hanging on the crosses to hasten their deaths in time for their bodies to be transported to graves before the Sabbath began. But John noted that when the soldiers got to Jesus, he was already dead, and therefore, they did not break his bones.

> These things happened *so that the scripture would be fulfilled:* "Not one of his bones will be broken," and, as another scripture says, *"They will look on the one they have pierced."*[159]

John quoted from two Psalms as well as from the Old Testament Book of Zechariah. The first quote was Psalm 34:20, which noted that the Messiah's bones would not be broken.

> *He protects all his bones, not one of them will be broken.*[160]

The second quote was from Psalm 22, where the Psalmist complained about being mistreated and having his hands and feet pierced.

---

[158] John 19:28-29
[159] John 19:36-37
[160] Psalm 34:20

> Dogs surround me, a pack of villains encircles me;
> *they pierce my hands and my feet.*[161]

The third quote was from Zechariah 12.

> And I will pour out on the house of David and the inhabitants of Jerusalem a spirit of grace and supplication. *They will look on me, the one they have pierced*, and they will mourn for him as one mourns for an only child, and grieve bitterly for him as one grieves for a firstborn son.[162]

As we have seen, John relied on historical precedent, telling us that Old Testament writers foretold the Messiah hundreds of years before Jesus came. John further noted that Jesus fulfilled all that the Old Testament writers foretold concerning the Messiah. Therefore, Jesus must be the Messiah.

---

161 Psalm 22:16

162 Zechariah 12:10

10 The Testimony of God

The Testimony of God the Father (John 5)

It is impossible to require God to testify in a trial. Nevertheless, John included God in his list of witnesses to testify. Jesus' words in John 5 referenced God's testimony.

> I have testimony weightier than that of John. For the very work that the Father has given me to finish, and which I am doing, testifies that the Father has sent me. And *the Father who sent me has himself testified concerning me.*[163]

Earlier in John's Gospel, John the Baptizer quoted God identifying Jesus as the one who will baptize with the Holy Spirit.

> I myself did not know him, but *the one who sent me to baptize with water told me, "The man on whom you see the Spirit come down and remain is the one who will baptize with the Holy Spirit."*[164]

John did not record the baptism of Jesus; only Matthew, Mark, and Luke recorded it. Although not a part of John, God's affirmation of Jesus at his baptism in Matthew 3:17, is noteworthy.

---

[163] John 5:36-37
[164] John 1:33

> And a voice from heaven said, "*This is my Son, whom I love; with him I am well pleased.*"[165]

The Testimony of God the Holy Spirit (John 14-16)

The Holy Spirit played a prominent role in the Gospel of John. The writer spent three chapters (John 14-16) discussing the Holy Spirit's role in the life of the believer. In John 14:7, Jesus called the Holy Spirit the Spirit of truth. The Holy Spirit's responsibility in the life of the believer is to convict of sin, glorify the person of Jesus, and transform believers into the image of the Lord Jesus Christ.[166] In John 15:26, Jesus highlighted the future ministry of the Holy Spirit. Jesus referred to the Spirit as 'the Counselor' (*paracletos*) who would originate with God the Father, would be sent to Christ's followers, and would testify concerning Jesus.

> When the Counselor comes, whom I will send to you from the Father, the Spirit of truth who goes out from the Father, *he will testify about me.*[167]

John 16 tells us that Jesus' disciples were not ready for all that Jesus wanted to say to them. But Jesus promised his disciples that the Holy Spirit would guide them to the truth, and that the Spirit would relate to them all they needed to know as they became ready to hear it.

> I have much more to say to you, more than you can now bear. *But when he, the Spirit of truth, comes, he will guide you into all the truth. He will not speak on his own; he will speak only what he hears, and he will tell you what is yet to come. He will glorify me because it is from me that he will receive what he will make known to you. All that belongs to the Father is mine. That is why I said the Spirit will receive from me what he will make known to you.*[168]

---

[165] Matthew 3:17

[166] http://blogs.blueletterbible.org/blb/2013/03/05/the-work-and-person-of-the-holy-spirit-in-the-gospel-of-john/

[167] John 15:26

[168] John 16:12-15

11 Calling the Defendant to Testify

The Testimony of God the Son

Putting a defendant on the witness stand can be risky. In most criminal trials, the defendant does not take the stand because he or she usually does not hold up well under cross-examination. The opposing attorney can make the defendant look really bad. Prosecutors dream of facing a defendant in court, of getting to ask him or her questions under cross-examination. An effective prosecutor can make a defendant squirm, sweat, slump, and sometimes even scream while on the stand. On the other hand, if the defendant does not testify, then it looks like guilt is being covered up.

In the case of *State of Florida v. George Zimmerman*, George Zimmerman was charged with second-degree murder stemming from the neighborhood shooting of Trayvon Martin on February 26, 2012. Before the trial concluded, Judge Debra Nelson asked Zimmerman if he had made a decision about taking the stand in his own defense. Zimmerman replied, "After consulting with counsel, [I've decided] not to testify, your Honor."[169] Zimmerman was acquitted.

On March 12, 2009, financier and former NASDAQ chairman Bernard Madoff pled guilty to eleven federal crimes and admitted to operating the largest Ponzi scheme in history. He was sentenced to 150 years in prison with restitution of $17 billion. Prosecutors estimated the size of the fraud to

[169]http://www.cnn.com/2013/07/10/justice/zimmerman-trial/

be $64.8 billion, based on the amounts in the accounts of Madoff's 4,800 clients as of November 30, 2008.[170]

Investigators determined that Madoff did not act alone. They alleged that at least five others were involved in the scheme. Of those, two—Daniel Bonventre, Madoff's former operations manager, and executive assistant Annette Bongiorno—testified in their own defense. On the witness stand, Bonventre told a jury that he respected and trusted Madoff for more than 40 years, until the latter's 2008 confession to masterminding the Ponzi scheme. Bonventre had earlier opted not to testify at his trial, but reversed his decision, saying, "My view changed at that moment. Now I think he's a terribly ill man, and it's difficult to reconcile everything I knew about him for 40 years and what I know now."[171] Although Bonventre denied all allegations against himself, his testimony backfired. The jury convicted him and the four other conspirators of fraud.

John decided to put Jesus on the witness stand in spite of the fact that he knew the religious leaders would try to make Jesus look foolish. That John would put Jesus on the witness stand is ironic because in John 5:31, Jesus said, "If I testify about myself, my testimony is not true." What Jesus meant by this statement is not clear. Certainly, Jesus never said anything that was not true. Perhaps, he was making a sarcastic statement referring to the fact that there was nothing he could say that would satisfy the religious leaders. They had already made up their minds to not believe Jesus' words about himself. Whatever the case, John called Jesus to the witness stand, asking Jesus one question over and over again: "Who do you say that you are?"

In answer to this question, John quoted Jesus on nine different occasions answering, "I am." In the Gospels, the phrase "I am" is only used in John. The phrase immediately takes us back to Mount Sinai when Moses asked God his name.[172] God said, "Tell them 'I Am' has sent you." By responding with this phrase, Jesus equated himself with God. Each "I Am" statement is followed by metaphors which express Jesus' saving relationship toward the world.

170http://online.wsj.com/news/articles/SB123685693449906551?mod=djemalertNEWS&mg=reno64-wsj&url=http%3A%2F%2Fonline.wsj.com%2Farticle%2FSB123685693449906551.html%3Fmod%3DdjemalertNEWS

171http://www.usatoday.com/story/money/business/2014/02/18/madoff-trial-bonventre/5580935/

172 Exodus 3:12-14

I AM the bread of life.

In John 6:35, Jesus declared,

> "I am the bread of life. He who comes to me will never go hungry, and he who believes in me will never be thirsty."[173]

In verse 48, Jesus said again, "I am the bread of life." These declarations come on the heels of John 6:1-13, where Jesus miraculously fed over five thousand people with five barley loaves and two fish. After feeding the multitudes, Jesus and his disciples crossed back to the other side of the Sea of Galilee. When the crowd discovered that Jesus had left, they followed him to Galilee. At this point, Jesus took the opportunity to teach them a lesson about the kind of bread he was offering them. He accused the crowd of following him only for the free meal, and then urged them to seek that which is far more lasting than physical bread. Jesus told them in John 6:26-27,

> Very truly I tell you, you are looking for me, not because you saw the signs I performed but because you ate the loaves and had your fill. Do not work for food that spoils, but for food that endures to eternal life, which the Son of Man will give you. For on him God the Father has placed his seal of approval.[174]

In other words, the crowds were so focused on the food that they missed out on the fact that the Messiah had come. Jesus went on to tell them that they needed to ask for the true bread from heaven that gives life. When they asked Jesus for this bread, he responded, "I am the bread of life; he who comes to me will never go hungry."

This is a remarkable statement by Jesus. First, by equating himself with bread, Jesus was saying that he is essential for life. Second, the life Jesus referred to was not physical life, but eternal life. The people needed to look beyond the physical so that they could see the spiritual. Jesus was contrasting what he offered as their Messiah with the bread he provided for them the day before. The bread he provided for them on the previous day was physical bread that perishes. He, on the other hand, is spiritual bread that brings eternal life.

---

[173] John 6:35

[174] John 6:26-27

IT IS I (I AM); be not afraid.

In John 6:16-21, the disciples had gone out in a small ship on the Sea of Galilee, a small freshwater lake in northeast Israel. As often occurs on Galilee, a sudden storm flared up. Such storms erupt as the result of differences in temperatures between the seashore and the mountains that border the sea, especially on the east. The Sea of Galilee lies 680 feet below sea level. The adjacent hills rise up to altitudes of 2000 feet. These heights are a source of cool, dry air in contrast to the warm, moist air concentrated directly around the lake. The difference in height between the surrounding land and the sea causes substantial temperature and pressure changes, prompting strong winds to funnel through the hills and sweep into the lake. Because the Sea of Galilee is small, these winds often descend directly to the center of the lake with violent results. A storm can erupt quickly and without warning, leaving small boats caught out on the sea in immediate danger. John 6:19-20 tells us:

> When they had rowed about three or four miles, they saw Jesus approaching the boat, walking on the water; and they were frightened. But he said to them, "It is I; don't be afraid."[175]

The Greek phrase translated "It is I" is the same phrase that is translated "I am." Thus, Jesus is actually saying, "I Am; don't be afraid." Jesus was saying that he is the ever-present God in the midst of whatever storm people are facing. Therefore, we need not fear.

I AM the light of the world.

In John chapters 8 and 9, Jesus called himself the light of the world.

> When Jesus spoke again to the people, he said, "I am the light of the world. Whoever follows me will never walk in darkness, but will have the light of life."[176]

> "While I am in the world, I am the light of the world."[177]

---

[175] John 6:19-20

[176] John 8:12

[177] John 9:5

In the scriptures, light and sight are grouped together to provide an analogy about people's ability to see and recognize who Jesus was. Jesus is the light of the world who enables us to see the realities of life. An understanding of the relationship between eyesight and light makes the analogy clearer. Without light, there would be no sight. Our ability to see is the result of the complex interaction of light, eyes, and the brain. We are able to see because light from an object moves through space and reaches our eyes. Just as without light there would be no physical sight, so without Jesus, the light of the world, there would be no eternal sight. In Matthew's Gospel, Jesus highlighted the connection.

> The eye is the lamp of the body. If your eyes are healthy, your whole body will be full of light. But if your eyes are unhealthy, your whole body will be full of darkness. If then the light within you is darkness, how great is that darkness![178]

Jesus' statements in John 8 and 9 were sandwiched between two stories about people's ability or lack of ability to see and perceive. John chapter 7 ended with a debate among the religious leaders over Jesus' identity. The passage revealed their inability to see Jesus for who he really was: the son of God.

> Finally the temple guards went back to the chief priests and the Pharisees, who asked them, "Why didn't you bring him in?"
>
> "No one ever spoke the way this man does," the guards replied.
>
> "You mean he has deceived you also?" the Pharisees retorted. "Have any of the rulers or of the Pharisees believed in him? No! But this mob that knows nothing of the law—there is a curse on them."
>
> Nicodemus, who had gone to Jesus earlier and who was one of their own number, asked, "Does our law condemn a man without first hearing him to find out what he has been doing?"
>
> They replied, "Are you from Galilee, too? Look into it, and you will find that a prophet does not come out of Galilee."[179]

---

[178] Matthew 6:22-23

[179] John 7:45-52

Jesus' statement in chapter 9 was located within the story of the man who was born blind, but to whom Jesus gave the ability to see (see the sixth piece of physical evidence above). John placed these "I am the light of the world" statements in the context of the contrasting sight stories. Some people receive Jesus' light and can see; others do not receive Jesus' light and, though they think they can see, in reality, they cannot.

Before Abraham was, I AM

In John 8:31-59, John described a tense dialogue between Jesus and some antagonistic Jews. As noted earlier, this debate revolved around Abraham and whether Jesus or his critics had the best claim to Abraham. Verse 58 contains one of the "I Am" statements of Jesus.

> "I tell you the truth," Jesus answered,
> "before Abraham was born, I am!"[180]

On the surface, Jesus was stating that he existed before Abraham was even born. But even more important, Jesus was again equating himself with God. Jesus was before Abraham in more than mere birth order. Jesus is the "I Am."

I AM the door.

In John 10, Jesus turned to the life of a shepherd, a familiar picture to people of the Middle East. Using this metaphor, Jesus made two "I Am" statements. The first one was "I am the gate for the sheep."

> Therefore Jesus said again, "Very truly I tell you, I am the gate for the sheep. All who have come before me are thieves and robbers, but the sheep have not listened to them. I am the gate; whoever enters through me will be saved. They will come in and go out, and find pasture. The thief comes only to steal and kill and destroy; I have come that they may have life, and have it to the full."[181]

The gate (or door as the KJV translates it) served two purposes. First, it kept predators out of the sheep pen. Second, it was the only point of

[180] John 8:58
[181] John 10:7-10

entrance for the sheep. In this context, the sheep referred to Jesus' own followers. By saying that he was the gate for the sheep, Jesus contended that he is the protector of the sheep and the only way for the sheep to enter the sheepfold.

I AM the good shepherd.

The second "I Am" statement in John 10 continued the shepherd analogy, except that in this case, Jesus, in addition to being the gate of the sheepfold, is the good shepherd.

> "I am the good shepherd. The good shepherd lays down his life for the sheep. The hired hand is not the shepherd and does not own the sheep. So when he sees the wolf coming, he abandons the sheep and runs away. Then the wolf attacks the flock and scatters it. The man runs away because he is a hired hand and cares nothing for the sheep. I am the good shepherd; I know my sheep and my sheep know me— just as the Father knows me and I know the Father—and I lay down my life for the sheep. I have other sheep that are not of this sheep pen. I must bring them also. They too will listen to my voice, and there shall be one flock and one shepherd. The reason my Father loves me is that I lay down my life—only to take it up again."[182]

Throughout John 10, Jesus contrasted himself with the Pharisees, the most influential religious group of his day. Jesus compared them to a hired hand who cares little about the sheep. In verse 12, Jesus distinguished the hired hand from the true shepherd who stands willing to give up his life for the sheep. Because the main consideration of the hired hand was his own compensation, his concern was not for the sheep but for himself. As the true shepherd, Jesus cared for the sheep to the point of giving up his own life for the sheep.

I AM the resurrection and the life.

As we have already seen, the resurrection of Lazarus was one of the pieces of physical evidence presented by John in his case for Jesus. Lazarus and his two sisters, Mary and Martha, were close friends with Jesus. According to John 11, Lazarus had become deathly sick, prompting his sisters to send for Jesus, who

---

[182] John 10:11-17

was in Galilee at the time. Jesus waited two days before leaving for Lazarus' hometown of Bethany. When Jesus finally arrived in Bethany, Lazarus had died and been entombed for four days. As soon as Martha became aware of Jesus' arrival, she met Jesus with what appears to be a soft complaint:

> On his arrival, Jesus found that Lazarus had already been in the tomb for four days. Now Bethany was less than two miles from Jerusalem, and many Jews had come to Martha and Mary to comfort them in the loss of their brother. When Martha heard that Jesus was coming, she went out to meet him, but Mary stayed at home. "Lord, if you had been here, our brother would not have died."
>
> Jesus responded to her by saying, "Your brother will rise again."
>
> Martha answered, "I know he will rise again in the resurrection at the last day."[183]

In response to Martha's statement, Jesus proclaimed his sixth "I Am" statement:

> Jesus said to her, "I am the resurrection and the life.
> He who believes in me will live, even though he dies."[184]

Jesus' statement revealed him to be in control over both death and life. He had the power to resurrect people from the dead, and he had the power to give eternal life to people who put their trust in him.

I AM the way, the truth and the life.

The next "I Am" statement from Jesus is found in John chapter 14, which opened with Jesus comforting his disciples as he tried to explain to them the events that were about to take place regarding his death. Though the disciples did not understand all that Jesus was saying, they comprehended enough to know that their lives were about to change dramatically. This realization left them troubled.

> "Do not let your hearts be troubled. You believe in God; believe also in me. My Father's house has many rooms; if that

[183] John 11:17-24
[184] John 11:25

> were not so, would I have told you that I am going there to prepare a place for you? And if I go and prepare a place for you, I will come back and take you to be with me that you also may be where I am. You know the way to the place where I am going."
>
> Thomas said to him, "Lord, we don't know where you are going, so how can we know the way?"
>
> Jesus answered, "I am the way and the truth and the life. No one comes to the Father except through me."[185]

By saying that he is the way, the truth, and the life, Jesus identified himself as the pathway through which everyone must travel in order to enter the kingdom of Heaven.

I AM the true vine.

In the final "I Am" statement, Jesus compared himself and his relationship with his followers to a grape vine and its branches.

> I am the true vine, and my Father is the gardener. He cuts off every branch in me that bears no fruit, while every branch that does bear fruit he prunes so that it will be even more fruitful. You are already clean because of the word I have spoken to you. Remain in me, as I also remain in you. No branch can bear fruit by itself; it must remain in the vine. Neither can you bear fruit unless you remain in me.
>
> I am the vine; you are the branches. If you remain in me and I in you, you will bear much fruit; apart from me you can do nothing. If you do not remain in me, you are like a branch that is thrown away and withers; such branches are picked up, thrown into the fire and burned. If you remain in me and my words remain in you, ask whatever you wish, and it will be done for you. This is to my Father's glory, that you bear much fruit, showing yourselves to be my disciples.
>
> As the Father has loved me, so have I loved you. Now remain in my love.[186]

Grape vineyards were prominent in Palestine, thus providing a ready-made object lesson. Jesus called attention to the different components of the

[185] John 14:1-6
[186] John 15:1-9

grape vine: the farmer, the vine, the branches, and the fruit. Jesus identified God the Father as the farmer. He described himself as the vine. He identified his followers as the branches. While Jesus was vague about the designation of the fruit, we can assume that he was talking about the character and witness of his followers. To be fruitful, the branches must remain attached to the vine because the vine provides all the nutrients needed for the branches to bear fruit. In the same way, Christ's followers must abide in Jesus to produce the character and witness embodied in Jesus Christ.

In the courtroom, Jesus' testimony might resemble the following.

John:	Would you please state your name for the court?
Jesus:	I am Jesus the Christ.
John:	Jesus, do you understand that you are on trial, and that the people seated on this jury will make decisions based on the information shared in this trial?
Jesus:	I am aware of this, yes.
John:	In your own words, who do you say that you yourself are?
Jesus:	I am the bread of life. He who comes to me will never go hungry, and he who believes in me will never be thirsty.
John:	By the bread of life, are you saying that you will physically feed those who come to you?
Jesus:	The bread that I offer endures to eternal life. Whoever comes to me will never go hungry, and whoever believes in me will never be thirsty.
John:	What else can you tell the court about yourself?
Jesus:	I am the light of the world. Whoever follows me will never walk in darkness, but will have the light of life.

John: Are you talking about physical light, as though from the sun or a candle?

Jesus: I am speaking in spiritual terms, not physical terms. I am the light that illuminates the way to eternal life.

John: You know how revered our father Abraham is. What is your relationship to Abraham?

Jesus: I tell you the truth, before Abraham was born, I am!

John: What do you mean by that?

Jesus: I mean that long before Abraham was even born, I had already existed for all eternity. Furthermore, as great as Abraham was and is, I stand eternally before him because I am the eternal God.

John: What else would you have us know about yourself?

Jesus: I am the gate for the sheep. Very truly I tell you, all who have come before me are thieves and robbers, but the sheep have not listened to them. I am the gate; whoever enters through me will be saved. They will come in and go out, and find pasture. The thief comes only to steal and kill and destroy; I have come that they may have life, and have it to the full. I am also the good shepherd. The good shepherd lays down his life for the sheep. The hired hand is not the shepherd and does not own the sheep. So, when he sees the wolf coming, he abandons the sheep and runs away. Then the wolf attacks the flock and scatters it. The man runs away because he is a hired hand and cares nothing for the sheep. I know my sheep and my sheep know me.

John: Most of what you have told us here has to do with life. What can you tell us about your power over death?

Jesus: I am the resurrection and the life. He who believes in me will live, even though he dies. Also, I am the way and the truth and the life. No one comes to the Father except through me.

John: Anything else we should know?

Jesus: I think I have already told you all you need to know for now.

John: What would you say to someone who has heard your testimony, the testimonies of all your friends, seen the physical evidence, and yet still has doubts about you?

Jesus: I would say that if you are looking for the Messiah, I am he. I have told you these things, so that in me you may have peace. In this world you will have trouble. But I have overcome the world. I told you that I am he. Because some have seen me, they have believed; blessed are those who have not seen and yet have believed.

John: Thank you, Jesus. No further questions, your Honor.

12 The Prosecution's Cross-Examination of Jesus

The case against Jackie Selebi had captivated South Africa for three years, and once the trial began, the prosecutor was in no mood for clemency. Selebi was the nation's top police official who at one time had led Interpol, the International Criminal Police Organization. Selebi was on trial for alleged corruption. Although he had argued that his wife had accidentally shredded evidence, when he took the stand, his testimony was ripped apart by his interrogator.

"You know what this means?" the prosecutor said. "That you are arrogant and that you lie."

When the trial ended in 2010, Selebi was convicted and sentenced to 15 years. The prosecutor, Gerrie Nel, had earned the respect of prosecutors worldwide, forging a reputation for abrasive, in-your-face, cross-examination that earned him a new nickname: "the pit bull."[187]

Nel, a career prosecutor with more than 30 years of experience, is well-known in South Africa for taking on big cases.[188] He formerly served as head of the elite Directorate of Special Operations, also known as the Scorpions, in Gauteng, a province in South Africa. In 2014, Nel prosecuted the case of Oscar Pistorius, the world champion paralympic sprinter.

---

[187] http://www.nytimes.com/2014/04/14/world/africa/pistorius-murder-trial.html?rref=world/africa&module=Ribbon&version=context®ion=Header&action=click&contentCollection=Africa&pgtype=article

[188] http://www.iol.co.za/dailynews/opinion/gerrie-nel-a-man-on-a-mission-1.1650485#.U02FUSqF9OU

Pistorius stood trial for murdering his girlfriend, South African model and reality TV star Reeva Steenkamp, at his home in Pretoria, South Africa on Valentine's Day in 2013. Pistorius claimed he thought Steenkamp was an intruder and shot her out of self-defense, but Nel countered that Pistorius purposefully shot her during an argument.[189]

At one point in the trial, Nel produced a photograph of Ms. Steenkamp's head wounds, with brain tissue exposed, and demanded that Mr. Pistorius look at it.

> That's it — have a look, Mr. Pistorius. I know you don't want to, because you don't want to take responsibility, but it's time that you look at it. Take responsibility for what you've done, Mr. Pistorius.[190]

Journalist Mandy Wiener wrote *Killing Kebble*, a study of the murder case of South African mining magnate Brett Kebble, another big case prosecuted by Nel. Wiener said:

> Nel is a relentless prosecutor who argues with such intensity and sense of justice that it's apparent he is personally invested in his cases. For him, it's about the facts. He can be very cold and very ruthless.[191]
>
> "Once he smells blood, he does not stop," one co-worker said about Nel.[192]

Gerrie Nel is not the only interrogator with "pit bull" prosecution skills. The Gospels teach us that the religious leaders of Jesus' day were relentless in their own right. John 8:3-6 tell us that the experts in the Law

[189] http://ferrall.radio.cbssports.com/2014/04/14/heather-hansen-prosecutor-gerrie-nel-unstoppable-in-oscar-pistorius-case/

[190] http://www.nytimes.com/2014/04/14/world/africa/pistorius-murder-trial.html?rref=world/africa&module=Ribbon&version=context®ion=Header&action=click&contentCollection=Africa&pgtype=article

[191] http://www.nytimes.com/2014/04/14/world/africa/pistorius-murder-trial.html?emc=edit_th_20140414&nl=todaysheadlines&nlid=41302790%C2%A0&_r=0

[192] http://www.nytimes.com/2014/04/14/world/africa/pistorius-murder-trial.html

and the Pharisees hammered Jesus with questions meant to catch him in some slip of the tongue.

> The teachers of the law and the Pharisees brought in a woman caught in adultery. They made her stand before the group and said to Jesus, "Teacher, this woman was caught in the act of adultery. In the Law Moses commanded us to stone such women. Now what do you say?" They were using this question as a trap, in order to have a basis for accusing him.[193]

As we have seen, John called Jesus, the defendant, to the witness stand even though putting a defendant on the witness stand is a risky decision. On the one hand, if the defendant does not testify, then he comes across as covering up guilt. On the other hand, if you put the defendant on the witness stand, there is the chance that the opposing attorney can make the defendant look really bad. John's questioning of Jesus was immediately followed by a cross-examination using the questions posed by the Pharisees. In their cross-examination, the Pharisees challenged Jesus' testimony, legitimacy, and his identity.

The religious leaders challenged Jesus' testimony.

Jesus' own testimony was one of the most powerful parts of John's case. But the religious leaders sought to discredit Jesus' testimony by declaring that it was not valid.

> The Pharisees challenged him, *"Here you are, appearing as your own witness; your testimony is not valid."*
>
> Jesus answered, "Even if I testify on my own behalf, my testimony is valid, for I know where I came from and where I am going. But you have no idea where I come from or where I am going. You judge by human standards; I pass judgment on no one. But if I do judge, my decisions are true, because I am not alone. I stand with the Father, who sent me. In your own Law it is written that the testimony of two witnesses is true. I am one who testifies for myself; my other witness is the Father, who sent me."[194]

---

[193] John 8:3-6
[194] John 8:13-18

The religious leaders challenged the legitimacy of Jesus' birth. Unlike Matthew and Luke, John did not include the virgin birth in his narrative. In spite of this, the virgin birth of Jesus persisted in the background throughout John's Gospel as John portrayed Jesus to be the son of God as opposed to the son of Joseph. Jesus' opponents used this storyline to attack the legitimacy of Jesus' birth and therefore his lineage, questioning whether Jesus was a full-blooded Jew, an important factor for any Jewish male in order to establish his Jewish identity.

> Then they asked him, *"Where is your father?"*
>
> "You do not know me or my Father," Jesus replied. "If you knew me, you would know my Father also." He spoke these words while teaching in the temple courts near the place where the offerings were put. Yet no one seized him, because his hour had not yet come.
>
> Once more Jesus said to them, "I am going away, and you will look for me, and you will die in your sin. Where I go, you cannot come."
>
> This made the Jews ask, *"Will he kill himself? Is that why he says, 'Where I go, you cannot come'?"*
>
> But he continued, "You are from below; I am from above. You are of this world; I am not of this world. I told you that you would die in your sins; if you do not believe that I am he, you will indeed die in your sins."
>
> *"Who are you?"* they asked.
>
> "Just what I have been telling you from the beginning," Jesus replied. "I have much to say in judgment of you. But he who sent me is trustworthy, and what I have heard from him I tell the world."
>
> They did not understand that he was telling them about his Father. So Jesus said, "When you have lifted up the Son of Man, then you will know that I am he and that I do nothing on my own but speak just what the Father has taught me. The one who sent me is with me; he has not left me alone, for I always do what pleases him." Even as he spoke, many believed in him.
>
> To the Jews who had believed him, Jesus said, "If you hold to my teaching, you are really my disciples. Then you will know the truth, and the truth will set you free."

They answered him, *"We are Abraham's descendants and have never been slaves of anyone. How can you say that we shall be set free?"*

Jesus replied, "Very truly I tell you, everyone who sins is a slave to sin. Now a slave has no permanent place in the family, but a son belongs to it forever. So if the Son sets you free, you will be free indeed. I know that you are Abraham's descendants. Yet you are looking for a way to kill me, because you have no room for my word. I am telling you what I have seen in the Father's presence, and you are doing what you have heard from your father."

"Abraham is our father," they answered.

"If you were Abraham's children," said Jesus, "then you would do what Abraham did. As it is, you are looking for a way to kill me, a man who has told you the truth that I heard from God. Abraham did not do such things. You are doing the works of your own father."

"We are not illegitimate children," they protested. *"The only Father we have is God himself."*

Jesus said to them, "If God were your Father, you would love me, for I have come here from God. I have not come on my own; God sent me. Why is my language not clear to you? Because you are unable to hear what I say. You belong to your father, the devil, and you want to carry out your father's desires. He was a murderer from the beginning, not holding to the truth, for there is no truth in him. When he lies, he speaks his native language, for he is a liar and the father of lies. Yet because I tell the truth, you do not believe me!

Can any of you prove me guilty of sin? If I am telling the truth, why don't you believe me? Whoever belongs to God hears what God says. The reason you do not hear is that you do not belong to God."

The Jews answered him, *"Aren't we right in saying that you are a Samaritan and demon-possessed?"*

"I am not possessed by a demon," said Jesus, "but I honor my Father and you dishonor me. I am not seeking glory for myself; but there is one who seeks it, and he is the judge. Very truly I tell you, whoever obeys my word will never see death."

At this they exclaimed, *"Now we know that you are demon-possessed! Abraham died and so did the prophets, yet you say that whoever obeys your word will never taste death. Are you greater than our father Abraham? He died, and so did the prophets. Who do you think you are?"*

> Jesus replied, "If I glorify myself, my glory means nothing. My Father, whom you claim as your God, is the one who glorifies me. Though you do not know him, I know him. If I said I did not, I would be a liar like you, but I do know him and obey his word. Your father Abraham rejoiced at the thought of seeing my day; he saw it and was glad."
>
> *"You are not yet fifty years old,"* they said to him, *"and you have seen Abraham!"*
>
> "Very truly I tell you," Jesus answered, "before Abraham was born, I am!" At this, they picked up stones to stone him, but Jesus hid himself, slipping away from the temple grounds.[195]

The religious leaders challenged Jesus' identity.

More than any other Gospel, John claimed Jesus to be not only the Son of God, but God himself. It was this claim that riled the religious leaders the most.

The Pharisees continued their inquisition in chapter 10.

> Then came the Feast of Dedication at Jerusalem. It was winter, and Jesus was in the temple area walking in Solomon's Colonnade. The Jews gathered around him, saying, *"How long will you keep us in suspense? If you are the Christ, tell us plainly."*
>
> Jesus answered, "I did tell you, but you do not believe. The works I do in my Father's name testify about me, but you do not believe because you are not my sheep. My sheep listen to my voice; I know them, and they follow me. I give them eternal life, and they shall never perish; no one will snatch them out of my hand. My Father, who has given them to me, is greater than all; no one can snatch them out of my Father's hand. I and the Father are one."
>
> Again his Jewish opponents picked up stones to stone him, but Jesus said to them, "I have shown you many good works from the Father. For which of these do you stone me?"
>
> *"We are not stoning you for any good work,"* they replied, *"but for blasphemy, because you, a mere man, claim to be God."*[196]

[195] John 8:19-59

[196] John 10:22-33

Using the italicized words from the scripture passages above as the basis for the prosecutor's questions, the cross-examination of Jesus might look like the following:

Prosecutor Shaytan Kakos:	So, we meet again, Jesus of Nazareth!
Jesus:	Indeed, we do, Shaytan.
Prosecutor Shaytan Kakos:	Well, here you are appearing as your own witness! You do know that your testimony is not valid, do you not?
Jesus:	Even if I testify on my own behalf, my testimony is valid, for I know where I came from and where I am going. But you have no idea where I come from or where I am going. You judge by human standards; I pass judgment on no one. But if I do judge, my decisions are true, because I am not alone. I stand with the Father, who sent me. In your own Law it is written that the testimony of two witnesses is true. I am one who testifies for myself; my other witness is the Father, who sent me.
Prosecutor Shaytan Kakos:	Where is your father? Can you bring him in to testify?
Jesus:	You know neither me nor my Father.
Prosecutor Shaytan Kakos:	You are right about that! We do not know your father. No one knows truly who your father was. Why, I bet even you are not sure about who your true father was! Is it not true that your mother was pregnant before she was ever married? That you were born out of wedlock?
Jesus:	If you knew me, you would know my Father also.
Prosecutor Shaytan Kakos:	Oh, I forgot that you never directly answer questions, do you Jesus? That

way, you do not have to answer for anything, do you? Well, friend, you are in a court of law today, and therefore you must answer the questions posed to you! Furthermore, you will not go anywhere until you do!

Jesus: I am going away, and you will look for me, and you will die in your sin. Where I go, you cannot come.

Prosecutor Shaytan Kakos: What do you mean when you say you are going away and we cannot find you? Will you kill yourself? Is that why you say, 'Where I go, you cannot come'?

Jesus: You are from below; I am from above. You are of this world; I am not of this world. I told you that you would die in your sins; if you do not believe that I am he, you will indeed die in your sins.

Prosecutor Shaytan Kakos: We will die in our sins? Seriously? Who do you think you are?

Jesus: Just what I have been telling you from the beginning. I have much to say in judgment of you.

Prosecutor Shaytan Kakos: You have much to say in judgment of us? My friend, *you* are the one on whom judgment will be passed in this court! You earlier said that you pass judgment on no one! Which is it, do you pass judgment or do you not pass judgment?

Jesus: You bring judgment on yourselves. That is why I say that I have much to say in judgment of you. But he who sent me is trustworthy, and what I have heard from him I tell the world.

Prosecutor Shaytan Kakos: What on earth does that mean? "He who sent me is trustworthy." You make no sense whatsoever!

Jesus:	When you have lifted up the Son of Man, then you will know that I am he and that I do nothing on my own but speak just what the Father has taught me. The one who sent me is with me; he has not left me alone, for I always do what pleases him. If you hold to my teaching, you are really my disciples. Then you will know the truth, and the truth will set you free.
Prosecutor Shaytan Kakos:	Sir, I do not know who you think you are, but, as for us, we are Abraham's descendants and have never been slaves of anyone. How can you say that we shall be set free?
Jesus:	Very truly I tell you, everyone who sins is a slave to sin. Now a slave has no permanent place in the family, but a son belongs to it forever. So if the Son sets you free, you will be free indeed. I know that you are Abraham's descendants. Yet you are looking for a way to kill me, because you have no room for my word. I am telling you what I have seen in the Father's presence, and you are doing what you have heard from your father.
Prosecutor Shaytan Kakos:	Abraham is our father!
Jesus:	If you were Abraham's children, then you would do what Abraham did. As it is, you are looking for a way to kill me, a man who has told you the truth that I heard from God. Abraham did not do such things. You are doing the works of your own father.
Prosecutor Shaytan Kakos:	Well, at least we have a father! We are not illegitimate children, which, from

what I have heard, is more than I can say for you, Jesus of Nazareth! The only Father we have is God himself.

Jesus: If God were your Father, you would love me, for I have come here from God. I have not come on my own; God sent me. Why is my language not clear to you? Is it because you are unable to hear what I say? You belong to your father, the devil, and you want to carry out your father's desires.

(At this statement, Shaytan Kakos shot Jesus a conniving look.)

He was a murderer from the beginning, not holding to the truth, for there is no truth in him. When he lies, he speaks his native language, for he is a liar and the father of lies.

Prosecutor Shaytan Kakos: What do you know of the devil, Jesus of Nazareth? You would not know the truth if it hit you squarely in the face!

Jesus: I know the truth about the devil even if his questions hit me squarely in the face. Get behind me, Shaytan!

Prosecutor Shaytan Kakos: Answer the questions, Jesus of Nazareth! We are here looking for the truth!

Jesus: I am telling the truth, yet you do not believe me! My word is truth. Can any of you prove me guilty of sin? If I am telling the truth, why do you not believe me? Whoever belongs to God hears what God says. The reason you do not hear is that you do not belong to God.

Prosecutor Shaytan Kakos: Are we not correct in saying that you are a Samaritan, half Gentile, and therefore cannot possibly be the

	Messiah since the Messiah must come from the family tree of David?
Jesus:	Again, you know neither me nor my father. God is my father.
Prosecutor Shaytan Kakos:	You sound like someone who is demon-possessed! Admit it! You are demon-possessed! Just admit it!
Jesus:	I am not possessed by a demon, but I honor my Father, whereas you dishonor me. I am not seeking glory for myself; but there is one who seeks it, and he is the judge. Very truly I tell you, whoever obeys my word will never see death.
Prosecutor Shaytan Kakos:	Now we know that you are demon-possessed! Abraham died and so did the prophets, yet you say that whoever obeys your word will never taste death. Are you greater than our father Abraham? He died, and so did the prophets. Who do you think you are?
Jesus:	You of all people should know, Mr. Shaytan Kakos, that I am not possessed by a demon. If I glorify myself, my glory means nothing. My Father, whom you claim as your God, is the one who glorifies me. Though you do not know him, I know him. If I said I did not, I would be a liar like you, but I do know him and obey his word. Your father Abraham rejoiced at the thought of seeing my day; he saw it and was glad.
Prosecutor Shaytan Kakos:	You are not yet fifty years old, and you have seen Abraham!
Jesus:	Very truly I tell you, before Abraham was born, I am!
Prosecutor Shaytan Kakos:	Ladies and gentlemen of the jury, this statement alone which you yourselves

have heard right out of this man's mouth is more than enough to find him guilty of blasphemy! What are we waiting for? Why not just go ahead and give this man what he deserves? Stone this man now!

With this exchange, the courtroom erupted into chaos forcing the judge to use his gavel while struggling to bring the trial to order. Finally, the judge called for a temporary recess to restore calm to the courtroom. When the trial resumed, the prosecution continued with the cross-examination of Jesus.

Prosecutor Shaytan Kakos: How long will you keep us in suspense with your circular reasoning? If you are the Christ, tell us plainly.

Jesus: I did tell you, but you do not believe. The works I do in my Father's name testify about me, but you do not believe because you are not my sheep. My sheep listen to my voice; I know them, and they follow me. I give them eternal life, and they shall never perish; no one will snatch them out of my hand. My Father, who has given them to me, is greater than all; no one can snatch them out of my Father's hand. I and the Father are one.

Upon hearing Jesus' words, the courtroom again erupted into disorder with some people standing, pointing their fingers at Jesus, and others making the mock motion of hurling stones toward him. The judge pounded his gavel to silence the courtroom.

Judge: Any further outbursts and I will clear this courtroom for the remainder of this trial! I will not tolerate chaos in my courtroom! Now, am I understood?

John: Your Honor, I apologize for interrupting, but may I please approach the bench?

Judge: Very well. *(Then to Shaytan Kakos)* Counselor?

(John and Shaytan Kakos walk to the front of the Judge's stand.)

Judge: *(To John)* What is it, counselor?

John: Your Honor, I would like to ask for another recess. I need to confer with my client.

Judge: We just finished a recess! And now you want another?

John: I know, and I apologize.

Judge: Can this recess wait at least until after the prosecution has concluded its cross-examination of your client?

John: Your Honor, my client's answers to the prosecution's cross-examination are exactly what I need to consult with him about!

Prosecutor Shaytan Kakos: Oh, well then! By all means, we need to recess! Maybe you can talk some sense into your client and instruct him to give clear answers to our questions! He is certainly doing himself no favors avoiding every question we ask. His answers are nonsensical! And the jury knows it!

John: Please, your Honor!

Judge: Very well. But you had best make good use of this one, counselor. You will not get another!

John: Thank you, your Honor.

(The two attorneys retreat to their desks.)

Judge: Court will recess until tomorrow morning at 9:00 a.m. I admonish the jury not to discuss this case among yourselves or with anyone else. Please keep an open mind and do not express or formulate any opinion as to a verdict regarding this defendant until this case is submitted to you for your final determination. Be back here tomorrow morning at 9 o'clock.

(John meets with his client in an upper conference room. As John and Jesus sit down, they hear a knock on the door. When the door opens, Simon Peter and Thomas enter the conference room and sit down with them.)

John: *(To Jesus)* Lord, what are you doing?

Jesus: What do you mean?

John: I mean that you are not answering the questions. You are being evasive, not making any sense.

Jesus: So you want me to give them the answers they are looking for?

John: I am just saying that you need to help yourself here! The jury will interpret your evasiveness as hiding something. You need to give clear answers, not vague answers.

Jesus: I only answer what my Father tells me to answer.

John: Lord, with all due respect, you are not doing yourself any favors here! I understand your reluctance to answer Kakos' questions, but you must be clear enough in your responses that the jury will empathize with you.

Simon Peter: Lord, *(glancing first at John)* if I may interject here. I have to agree with John. I think the jury is confused by your answers to the prosecution's questions. If you spoke more clearly, I believe you would fare better.

Jesus: So are you an expert witness now, Simon? You do not get it, do you?

John: Get what? What do you mean?

Jesus: I am not here to be ministered to, but to minister. Neither am I here to advocate for myself, but to advocate for others and to give my life as a sacrifice for others. This is the reason I came, to be tried and killed, and then—

Simon Peter: Never, Lord! This should never happen to you!

Jesus *(mumbling)*: Get behind me…

Simon Peter: Pardon me? What did you say?

Jesus: I said, 'Get behind me Satan,' for you are a hindrance to me. You are seeing things merely from a human point of view, not from God's point of view.

Thomas: Lord, forgive me for interrupting, but John and Peter are right. Do you remember when we began following you? You spoke in metaphors and parables that were hard for us to understand. But later on, you began speaking more clearly, not using figures of speech. It was then that we came to realize that you knew all things, and that you had no need for anyone to question you. It was only when you spoke plainly that we became absolutely convinced that you came from God.

Jesus: Gentlemen, you have believed because you have seen me, spent time with me, talked with me, fellowshipped with me. But the time will come when the more blessed person will be the one who believes in me even though they have spent no time with me, never audibly heard me speak. Blessed are they who believe in me though they have not seen.

John: Lord, please, you must help this jury to see!

Jesus: This generation is a wicked generation; it seeks for a sign, and yet no sign will be given to it but the sign of Jonah. For just as Jonah became a sign to the Ninevites, so will the Son of Man be to this generation. Do you believe this?

John: Lord, we, the three of us, are not the ones who need convincing. Help us help you by convincing the jury!

Jesus: You do not know what you are asking. Are you able to drink the cup that I am about to drink?

Simon Peter: Lord, we would lay down our lives for you!

Jesus: I will not say much more to you, for the prince of this world is coming. He has no hold over me, but he comes so that the world may learn that I love the Father and do exactly what my Father has commanded me. Come now; let us leave. The jury waits.

John: Very well, then. I guess there is nothing more we can say.

Thomas: Yes. Let us also go, that we may die with him.

Back in the courtroom on the following day, Prosecutor Shaytan Kakos is restless, hoping that whatever conversation John had with his client will result in Jesus giving more straightforward answers to his interrogations. The dark circles under John's eyes betray his frustration with the course of the case. Jesus' disciples sit wearily in the back of the courtroom, their fingers tapping.

Prosecutor Shaytan Kakos:	Well, Jesus of Nazareth! Are you ready now to give some real answers to our questions? Or will you continue this charade of avoiding every question we ask?
Jesus:	I have not spoken on my own, but the Father who sent me commanded me to say all that I have spoken.
Prosecutor Shaytan Kakos:	Well, some father you have! If your father were indeed God as you say (which I seriously doubt!), then I think your father would have you answer more understandably than you have.
Jesus:	If you say so.
Prosecutor Shaytan Kakos:	Oh my dear Jesus! I think you have been your own worst enemy here, Jesus *so-called* the Christ! Once again, your testimony is not valid. Your own words incriminate you! You deserve to be stoned!
Jesus:	I have shown you many good works from the Father. For which of these do you wish to stone me?
Prosecutor Shaytan Kakos:	We would not stone you for any good work, but for blasphemy, because you, a mere man, claim to be God.
Jesus:	Is it not written in your Law, 'I have said you are "gods"'? If he called them 'gods,' to whom the word of God came—and Scripture cannot be set

	aside—what about the one whom the Father set apart as his very own and sent into the world? Why then do you accuse me of blasphemy because I said, 'I am God's Son'? Do not believe me unless I do the works of my Father. But if I do them, even though you do not believe me, at least believe the works that I do, that you may know and understand that the Father is in me, and I in the Father.
Prosecutor Shaytan Kakos:	You, sir, are an imposter! Oh, I think we have heard enough here! I have no further questions for this poor excuse of a witness, your Honor. This blasphemous rambler may step down!

At the end of the cross-examination, John 8:30 stands out as amazing. It noted, "Even as he spoke, many believed in him." It appeared that in spite of the rigorous cross-examination, people still believed in Jesus. Even then, as John gazed upon the faces of the jurors, it was hard to tell who was fully convinced and who remained to be convinced. John tried to break a smile through his uneasiness.

13 The Final Piece of Physical Evidence

It was the last piece of evidence, and the most important: a timeworn phone receipt from a Quality Inn in Orlando, Florida that would have proven Jonathan Fleming's innocence. But the arresting officers and investigators overlooked it.

In 1990 a New York court convicted Fleming of the August 15, 1989 killing of a drug dealer named Darryl Alston, also known as Darryl "Black" Rush, at a housing development in Brooklyn, New York. Fleming insisted that he was in Orlando at the time of the shooting, on a family trip to Walt Disney World. During the trial, Mr. Fleming's lawyers presented evidence, plane tickets, video footage, and vacation photos from family members, showing that Fleming was in Orlando around the time of the murder. But prosecutors countered, arguing that Fleming could have returned to Brooklyn, where his car was used in the shooting, and then flown back to Orlando.[197] Prosecutors produced a list of 53 possible flights Fleming could have taken from Orlando to Brooklyn and back. Prosecutors also cast doubt on the testimony from Mr. Fleming's family members about Fleming's whereabouts at the time of the murder.

"The prosecutors at the time essentially argued to the jury that you shouldn't believe his family," one of Fleming's attorneys, Anthony Mayol, told *Newsweek*. "What they didn't turn over in addition to the phone receipts is a letter from the Orlando Police Department confirming he was down there. Those independent people who were not family members would

[197] http://www.newsweek.com/wrongfully-convicted-jonathan-fleming-freed-after-24-years-i-have-no-faith-system-245972

have undercut the district attorney's argument that, oh, you can't listen to his family."[198]

But prosecutors had an eyewitness!

Jacqueline Belardo, a crack addict, claimed she saw Jonathan Fleming murder Darryl Alston, though she recanted her statement at the time of the conviction. Before testifying at trial, Ms. Belardo said she told investigators she had lied, but they threatened to arrest her for perjury. The same thing happened again about a year later, she said. She stated that she had pointed out Mr. Fleming in exchange for a dismissal of grand larceny charges against her. The recantation surfaced during one of Mr. Fleming's appeal hearings, but the judge discounted her new testimony after the prosecution contended that Ms. Belardo's recantation was a lie. Jonathan Fleming would spend almost 25 years in prison, while the evidence that would have exonerated him sat unnoticed in his case file.[199]

In June 2013 Mr. Fleming's defense team asked the Brooklyn District Attorney's Office to review Mr. Fleming's case. In November, members of the Conviction Integrity Unit reviewed the file and turned over to the defense police logs they had discovered. The logs showed that authorities had brought in Ms. Belardo, the purported eyewitness, after she had been found in a stolen van, and charged her with grand larceny. After several hours of questioning, she identified Mr. Fleming as Alston's killer. A little over an hour later, authorities dropped the charges against Ms. Belardo and released her.

The review unit also turned over the phone receipt with a timestamp proving that Fleming could not have been in New York in time to gun down Alston. According to the receipt, at 9:27 p.m. on August 14, 1989, Mr. Fleming paid a phone bill at the Orlando Quality Inn, making it impossible that he could have made it back to Brooklyn in time for the 2:15 a.m. shooting on August 15. The receipt was not handed over to the defense and was not a part of trial evidence. Taylor Koss, another member of Fleming's defense team, said that Mr. Fleming had asked about the receipt at the time of the trial and that a detective at the trial was questioned about the receipt, but said he did not recall recovering it.

---

198 Ibid.

199 http://www.nytimes.com/2014/04/09/nyregion/brooklyn-district-attorney-overturns-conviction-in-1989-murder.html

Investigators in the review unit also found a report from the Orlando Police Department, which had looked into Mr. Fleming's alibi at the request of the New York Police Department. Orlando police officers had interviewed employees of the Quality Inn where Fleming was staying. The police report said several hotel staff members remembered seeing Fleming there. But at the trial, the only witnesses to vouch for Mr. Fleming's presence in Orlando were family members. Neither the phone receipt nor the testimony of the hotel staff was ever handed over to the defense. In addition to this evidence, the Conviction Integrity Unit also interviewed a former girlfriend of Fleming's who said she called Fleming on the night of the murder at his hotel. Phone records corroborated her story.[200] Taylor Koss told *the New York Post*, "[Prosecutors] had the evidence that this man was on a Disney World vacation when this crime was committed. It's disgusting."[201]

As part of their investigation, the defense and prosecutors re-interviewed witnesses to the murder, and their accounts pointed to a different suspect. Assistant district attorney Mark Hale admitted, "We, in looking at the evidence, do not believe we have the present ability to retry the defendant, nor will the office be able to retry him in the future."[202] On Tuesday, April 8, 2014, the man who spent almost a quarter-century behind bars for murder was freed and cleared of a killing that happened when he was 1,100 miles away on a Disney World vacation.

In presenting his case for Jesus, John saved his most important piece of physical evidence for last. He had already put forth overwhelming evidence to substantiate his claims that Jesus was the Messiah. For instance, how could anyone top the raising of Lazarus from the dead, especially after Lazarus had been in the tomb four days? But Jesus' last miraculous sign topped everything else John had written, including the raising of Lazarus. It is truly miraculous for someone to raise another person from the dead; but it is another thing altogether for a person to raise himself from the dead.

As in the case of Jonathan Fleming, John's last piece of physical evidence came with the testimony of eyewitnesses such as Mary Magdalene, Simon Peter, the disciple whom Jesus loved, Thomas, and the other disciples. But, unlike Jacqueline Belardo in the Fleming case, John's

---

[200] http://www.amny.com/news/jonathan-fleming-freed-after-24-years-in-prison-for-murder-he-didn-t-commit-1.7648146

[201] http://rt.com/usa/wrongly-convicted-released-hotel-recepit-277/

[202] http://www.nytimes.com/2014/04/09/nyregion/brooklyn-district-attorney-overturns-conviction-in-1989-murder.html

witnesses were credible and had nothing to recant. Most significantly, like the all-important phone receipt in the Fleming case, John's last and most important piece of evidence, the resurrection, went largely unnoticed. John described the greatest event in history in chapter 20.

> Early on the first day of the week, while it was still dark, Mary Magdalene went to the tomb and saw that the stone had been removed from the entrance. So she came running to Simon Peter and the other disciple, the one Jesus loved, and said, "They have taken the Lord out of the tomb, and we don't know where they have put him!"
>
> So Peter and the other disciple started for the tomb. Both were running, but the other disciple outran Peter and reached the tomb first. He bent over and looked in at the strips of linen lying there but did not go in. Then Simon Peter came along behind him and went straight into the tomb. He saw the strips of linen lying there, as well as the cloth that had been wrapped around Jesus' head. The cloth was still lying in its place, separate from the linen. Finally the other disciple, who had reached the tomb first, also went inside. He saw and believed. (They still did not understand from Scripture that Jesus had to rise from the dead.) Then the disciples went back to where they were staying.
>
> Now Mary stood outside the tomb crying. As she wept, she bent over to look into the tomb and saw two angels in white, seated where Jesus' body had been, one at the head and the other at the foot.
>
> They asked her, "Woman, why are you crying?"
>
> "They have taken my Lord away," she said, "and I don't know where they have put him." At this, she turned around and saw Jesus standing there, but she did not realize that it was Jesus.
>
> He asked her, "Woman, why are you crying? Who is it you are looking for?"
>
> Thinking he was the gardener, she said, "Sir, if you have carried him away, tell me where you have put him, and I will get him."
>
> Jesus said to her, "Mary."
>
> She turned toward him and cried out in Aramaic, "Rabboni!" (which means "Teacher").
>
> Jesus said, "Do not hold on to me, for I have not yet ascended to the Father. Go instead to my brothers and tell

> them, 'I am ascending to my Father and your Father, to my God and your God.'"
>
> Mary Magdalene went to the disciples with the news: "I have seen the Lord!" And she told them that he had said these things to her.
>
> On the evening of that first day of the week, when the disciples were together, with the doors locked for fear of the Jewish leaders, Jesus came and stood among them and said, "Peace be with you!" After he said this, he showed them his hands and side. The disciples were overjoyed when they saw the Lord.
>
> Again Jesus said, "Peace be with you! As the Father has sent me, I am sending you." And with that he breathed on them and said, "Receive the Holy Spirit. If you forgive anyone's sins, their sins are forgiven; if you do not forgive them, they are not forgiven."
>
> Now Thomas (also known as Didymus), one of the Twelve, was not with the disciples when Jesus came. So the other disciples told him, "We have seen the Lord!"
>
> But he said to them, "Unless I see the nail marks in his hands and put my finger where the nails were, and put my hand into his side, I will not believe."
>
> A week later his disciples were in the house again, and Thomas was with them. Though the doors were locked, Jesus came and stood among them and said, "Peace be with you!" Then he said to Thomas, "Put your finger here; see my hands. Reach out your hand and put it into my side. Stop doubting and believe."
>
> Thomas said to him, "My Lord and my God!"
>
> Then Jesus told him, "Because you have seen me, you have believed; blessed are those who have not seen and yet have believed."[203]

The significance of the resurrection of Jesus Christ cannot be overstated. Along with the crucifixion, the resurrection is the most important event in history. First, the resurrection of Christ was necessary to prove that Jesus was who he claimed to be. Jesus claimed to be the son of God, which was the reason the religious leaders conspired to kill him (John 19:7).

The resurrection is vital because it demonstrated that Christ was divine. The fact that Jesus Christ died on the cross does not prove in itself that

[203] John 20:1-29

Jesus is God. Jesus proved his deity by fulfilling the prophecies of his death and by his being raised from the grave. The Bible declares that Jesus "was shown to be the Son of God when he was raised from the dead by the power of the Holy Spirit. He is Jesus Christ our Lord."[204]

The resurrection is significant because it proved Christ's ability to forgive sin. The Apostle Paul said, "…if Christ has not been raised, your faith is futile; you are still in your sins."[205] By rising from the dead, Jesus proved his power to conquer sin and to assure forgiveness and eternal life to all who receive his gift of salvation.

The resurrection is important because it revealed Christ's power over death. The Bible records, "For we know that since Christ was raised from the dead, he cannot die again; death no longer has mastery over him."[206] The resurrection secured our victory over death as well because "God raised us up with Christ and seated us with him in the heavenly realms in Christ Jesus."[207]

Jesus' resurrection is crucial because it showed that physical death is not the termination of human life. Jesus' triumph over the grave is God's pledge to us that we too shall be raised. This is why Jesus is referred to as the "firstfruits of those who have fallen asleep."[208] Christianity hinges on the reality of the resurrection. For this reason, John brought to the stand people who confirmed that Jesus was buried, and who witnessed the resurrected Christ.

Joseph of Arimathea testified concerning Jesus. (John 19)

Joseph of Arimathea is mentioned in all four New Testament Gospels. He donated his own prepared tomb for the burial of Jesus after Jesus' crucifixion. According to Mark 15:43, Joseph was a "prominent member of the council," meaning a member of the Jewish Sanhedrin. Mark also listed Joseph among those "waiting for the kingdom of God." Matthew 27:57 described him as a rich man and a disciple of Jesus. According to John 19:38, Joseph was a disciple of Jesus, but secretly because he feared the Jewish leaders. Thus, he could have been among the leaders John earlier called to the witness stand, but who refused to testify because of a fear of retribution from the Pharisees. But now, Joseph is more open to testifying on Jesus' behalf.

---

[204] Romans 1:4 NLT

[205] 1 Corinthians 15:17

[206] Romans 6:9

[207] Ephesians 2:6

[208] 1 Corinthians 15:20

As soon as Joseph heard the news of Jesus' death, he approached Pilate for permission to take Jesus' body away. Once Pilate was assured that Jesus was dead, he granted Joseph's request. Luke's Gospel tells us that Joseph was a good and upright man who had not consented to the decision and action of his colleagues on the Sanhedrin (Luke 23:50-51).

Joseph purchased fine linen (Mark 15:46) and went to Golgotha to remove the body of Jesus from the cross. The following passage from John 19 describes what took place.

> Later, Joseph of Arimathea asked Pilate for the body of Jesus. Now Joseph was a disciple of Jesus, but secretly because he feared the Jews. With Pilate's permission, he came and took the body away. He was accompanied by Nicodemus, the man who earlier had visited Jesus at night. Nicodemus brought a mixture of myrrh and aloes, about seventy-five pounds. Taking Jesus' body, the two of them wrapped it, with the spices, in strips of linen. This was in accordance with Jewish burial customs. At the place where Jesus was crucified, there was a garden, and in the garden a new tomb, in which no one had ever been laid. Because it was the Jewish day of Preparation and since the tomb was nearby, they laid Jesus there.[209]

Joseph's words on the witness stand served two purposes: first, they reveal that a high ranking member of the Jewish Council believed in Jesus; and second, they confirm that Jesus' body was indeed entombed. Joseph's testimony might resemble the following:

John:	Please state your name and your occupation for the court.
Joseph of Arimathea:	I am Joseph of Arimathea. I am a member of the Jewish ruling council, known as the Sanhedrin.
John:	As a member of the Sanhedrin, you were present when the council voted to arrest and crucify Jesus?
Joseph of Arimathea:	I was present for the vote, although I voted against crucifying Jesus.

[209] John 19:38-42

John:	So you did not agree with crucifying Jesus Christ?
Joseph of Arimathea:	No, I did not.
John:	Please tell the court why you were opposed to crucifying Jesus.
Joseph of Arimathea:	I was opposed to crucifying Jesus because I did not believe Jesus committed any crime, especially any crime worthy of death.
John:	Is that the only reason you opposed Jesus' execution?
Joseph of Arimathea:	Since I first heard Jesus speak, I have been intrigued by him. I have never heard anyone speak as powerfully as he does. Plus, he showed himself able to do things no one else has ever done, to my knowledge.
John:	Were you a follower of Jesus?
Joseph of Arimathea:	Not at first, but, in time, I came to follow him, but secretly. Job security, you know.
John:	When Jesus was crucified, you arranged for his body to be buried in your own tomb. Tell us about that.
Joseph of Arimathea:	I discovered that Jesus had no burial place. I had a burial plot that I had prepared for myself when I die. I asked Pilate for permission to remove Jesus' body for burial. When Pilate consented, a friend and I took the body, anointed it with perfume, wrapped it in linen, and placed it in my tomb.
John:	So, you can confirm for us under oath that you entombed the body of Jesus in your own burial plot?
Joseph of Arimathea:	Yes, sir, that is correct.
John:	You said a friend helped you.

Joseph of Arimathea:	Yes.
John:	And that friend was—
Joseph of Arimathea:	Nicodemus.
John:	Nicodemus, the one who had visited Jesus at night?
Joseph of Arimathea:	Yes, that Nicodemus. We both had misgivings about the Sanhedrin's decision. We both had come to believe in Jesus, but neither of us had expressed our belief openly until after Jesus' execution. We both feared what our colleagues might do.
John:	So, you and Nicodemus, both members of the Sanhedrin, now believe Jesus to be the Christ?
Joseph of Arimathea:	We do.

Simon Peter was called to the witness stand.
(John 1:40-42; 6:68; 18:10-11, 15-18, 20-21, 25-27;)

The basis for Peter's courtroom testimony can be found in five places in John's Gospel supplemented by some helpful passages in Matthew, Mark, and Luke. Let's look at each of these passages, and then imagine what the combined testimony of Peter from the passages would look like.

The first text featuring Peter comes from John 1:40-42. As noted above, Andrew introduced his brother, Simon, to Jesus. Upon seeing Simon, Jesus revealed that he had prior knowledge of Simon, and then gave him a nickname, Cephas, an Aramaic term that means "a rock." In Greek, the word is "Petros," from which we get the English name "Peter."

> Jesus looked at him and said, "You are Simon son of John. You will be called Cephas" (which, when translated, is Peter).[210]

A portion of Peter's testimony can be found in John 6, a passage which showed Jesus' popularity deteriorating, and his followers leaving him in droves. Jesus turned to his inner circle of disciples, and asked, "You do not want to leave too, do you?"

---

[210] John 1:42

In verse 68, Simon Peter answered him,

> *Lord, to whom shall we go? You have the words of eternal life. We believe and know that you are the Holy One of God.*[211]

To the above response, we can add Matthew's record of Peter's encounter with Jesus, where Peter responded to Jesus' question concerning whom the disciples said Jesus is.

> When Jesus came to the region of Caesarea Philippi, he asked his disciples, "Who do people say the Son of Man is?"
>
> They replied, "Some say John the Baptist; others say Elijah; and still others, Jeremiah or one of the prophets."
>
> "But what about you?" he asked. "Who do you say I am?"
>
> Simon Peter answered, "*You are the Messiah, the Son of the living God.*"[212]

The third place to feature Peter in John's Gospel is chapter 18. In this chapter, John recorded the betrayal of Jesus by Judas Iscariot, the arrest of Jesus by Roman soldiers and religious officials, and the questioning of Jesus by Caiaphas, the High Priest, and Pontius Pilate. Also in this chapter, John described the low point in Simon Peter's life, when Peter denied that he knew Jesus.

> Simon Peter and another disciple were following Jesus. Because this disciple was known to the high priest, he went with Jesus into the high priest's courtyard, but Peter had to wait outside at the door. The other disciple, who was known to the high priest, came back, spoke to the servant girl on duty there and brought Peter in.
>
> "You aren't one of this man's disciples too, are you?" she asked Peter.
>
> He replied, "*I am not.*" It was cold, and the servants and officials stood around a fire they had made to keep warm. Peter also was standing with them, warming himself.
>
> Meanwhile, Simon Peter was still standing there warming himself. So they asked him, "You aren't one of his disciples too, are you?"

---

[211] John 6:68

[212] Matthew 15:13-16

> He denied it, saying, "*I am not.*"
>
> One of the high priest's servants, a relative of the man whose ear Peter had cut off, challenged him, "Didn't I see you with him in the garden?"
>
> Again Peter denied it, and at that moment a rooster began to crow.[213]

More of Peter's denial is found in the Gospels of Matthew and Luke. Below is Matthew's version:

> After a little while, those standing there went up to Peter and said, "Surely you are one of them; your accent gives you away."
>
> Then *he began to call down curses, and he swore to them, "I don't know the man!"*
>
> Immediately a rooster crowed. Then Peter remembered the word Jesus had spoken: "Before the rooster crows, you will disown me three times." And he went outside and wept bitterly.[214]

Luke described Peter's last denial.

> About an hour later another asserted, "Certainly this fellow was with him, for he is a Galilean."
>
> Peter replied, "*Man, I don't know what you're talking about!*"
>
> Just as he was speaking, the rooster crowed. The Lord turned and looked straight at Peter. Then Peter remembered the word the Lord had spoken to him: "Before the rooster crows today, you will disown me three times." And he went outside and wept bitterly.[215]

Peter's testimony can also be drawn from John 20. In this chapter, Peter testified to what he and another disciple discovered at the tomb on the day of the resurrection, and to having seen the risen Jesus. When Mary Magdalene discovered the empty tomb early that morning, she ran to tell the disciples. John described what Peter and an unnamed disciple did upon hearing Mary Magdalene's report.

---

[213] John 18:15-18, 25-27

[214] Matthew 26:73-75

[215] Luke 22:59-62

> So Peter and the other disciple started for the tomb. Both were running, but the other disciple outran Peter and reached the tomb first. He bent over and looked in at the strips of linen lying there but did not go in. Then Simon Peter, who was behind him, arrived and went into the tomb. He saw the strips of linen lying there, as well as the burial cloth that had been around Jesus' head. The cloth was folded up by itself, separate from the linen. Finally the other disciple, who had reached the tomb first, also went inside. He saw and believed.[216]

Later that same day, Jesus appeared to his disciples, who were barricaded in a locked room.

> On the evening of that first day of the week, when the disciples were together, with the doors locked for fear of the Jewish leaders, Jesus came and stood among them and said, "Peace be with you!" After he said this, he showed them his hands and side. The disciples were overjoyed when they saw the Lord.
>
> Again Jesus said, "Peace be with you! As the Father has sent me, I am sending you." And with that he breathed on them and said, "Receive the Holy Spirit. If you forgive anyone's sins, their sins are forgiven; if you do not forgive them, they are not forgiven."[217]

The final portion of Peter's testimony comes from John 21, a chapter added after the rest of John's Gospel was written. Though an addendum, John 21 is an invaluable part of John's Gospel because, in this chapter, Jesus restored Simon Peter. To jump straight from the Gospels to the Book of Acts, which clearly identifies Simon Peter as the leader of the remaining disciples, leaves one to wonder how Peter got to be the leader of the Twelve. John's concluding chapter answered that question.

The chapter opens with a post-resurrection scene on the Sea of Galilee. The disciples have returned to fishing. After having toiled some time without catching any fish, the disciples heard Jesus offering advice from the shore, though at first they did not recognize him. Jesus instructed them to hoist their nets on the other side of the boat, a picture reminiscent of the story in Luke 5. The disciples followed Jesus' instructions and immediately hauled in a

---

[216] John 20:3-8
[217] John 20:19-23

catch too large to handle. At that point, Simon Peter recognized Jesus, and led the fishermen in dragging the net to shore. After Jesus furnished breakfast for the group on the beach, he approached Simon Peter.

> When they had finished eating, Jesus said to Simon Peter, "Simon son of John, do you love me more than these?"
>
> "*Yes, Lord,*" he said, "*you know that I love you.*"
>
> Jesus said, "Feed my lambs."
>
> Again Jesus said, "Simon son of John, do you love me?"
>
> He answered, "*Yes, Lord, you know that I love you.*"
>
> Jesus said, "Take care of my sheep."
>
> The third time he said to him, "Simon son of John, do you love me?"
>
> Peter was hurt because Jesus asked him the third time, "Do you love me?" He said, "*Lord, you know all things; you know that I love you.*"
>
> Jesus said, "Feed my sheep. Very truly I tell you, when you were younger you dressed yourself and went where you wanted; but when you are old you will stretch out your hands, and someone else will dress you and lead you where you do not want to go." Jesus said this to indicate the kind of death by which Peter would glorify God. Then he said to him, "Follow me!"
>
> Peter turned and saw that the disciple whom Jesus loved was following them.[218]

In this situation, the number three plays a significant role. John reported that this was Jesus' third appearance to the disciples since his resurrection. Jesus asked Peter three questions to which Peter gave three responses. Scholars point out the connection between Jesus' threefold question and Peter's threefold denial of Christ (John 18:15-18, 25-27). The repeated question and answer is interpreted as symbolically undoing the repeated denial of Jesus. New Testament scholar Raymond Brown notes:

> There were three denials, and now three confessions, as well as three commissions. This is significant because it was Near Eastern custom to say something three times before witnesses in order to solemnize it.[219]

---

[218] John 21:15-20

[219] Raymond Brown. The Gospel According to John XIII-XXI (Anchor Bible, Vol. 29), Doubleday, p. 1112.

Peter's hurt after the third question was most likely due to the fact that it reminded him of his three denials. Added to this connection is the fact that Peter's denials in John 18, and his three responses to Jesus' questions in John 21, occurred by a campfire.

One textual issue regarding the dialogue between Jesus and Peter revolves around the translation from Greek to English. Most English translations do not differentiate between the two different Greek words for "love" that are in the text, *agape* and *phileo*. *Agape* means unconditional love, and is considered a deeper form of love than mere *phileo*, which denotes friendship and brotherly love. In English, both words are translated with the one word, love.

Jesus:	Do you *agapas* (agape) me more than these? ("Do you *love* me more than these?")
Simon Peter:	Lord, you know that I *phileo* you. ("You know that I *love* you.")
Jesus:	Do you *agapas* me? ("Do you *love* me?")
Simon Peter:	Lord, you know that I *phileo* you. ("You know that I *love* you.")
Jesus:	Do you *phileis* (phileo) me? ("Do you *love* me?")
Simon Peter:	Yes, Lord, I *phileo* you. ("I *love* you.")

Most interpreters do not make much of this linguistic difference. They see the two different Greek verbs as synonymous. However, a differentiation between the two verbs in this text reveals a new realism on the part of Simon Peter, and a remarkable willingness on the part of Jesus to meet Peter where he was. Peter realized that he could no longer afford to arrogantly promise more than he could deliver. Jesus, in his grace, offered to meet Peter where he was on his spiritual journey. In this case, a paraphrase of the conversation would sound like this:

> When they had finished eating, Jesus said to Simon Peter, "Simon son of John, do you love me more than anything else to the point of sacrificing everything for me?"

"Yes, Lord," he said, "you know that I feel for you like a brother."

Jesus said, "Feed my lambs."

Again Jesus said, "Simon son of John, do you love me more than anything else to the point of sacrificing everything for me?"

He answered, "Lord, I don't want to make the same mistake I did before, promising something, but failing to deliver. But you know that I feel for you as if you were my own brother."

Jesus said, "Take care of my sheep."

The third time he said to him, "Okay, Simon, so you love me as a brother?"

Peter was hurt because Jesus asked him a third time. He said, "Lord, you know all things; you know that I love you as my brother."

Jesus said, "Feed my sheep. Very truly I tell you, when you were younger you dressed yourself and went where you wanted; but when you are old you will stretch out your hands, and someone else will dress you and lead you where you do not want to go." Jesus said this to indicate the kind of death by which Peter would glorify God. Then he said to him, "Follow me!"

When we take all of the preceding passages related to Peter, and compile them into a courtroom dialogue, Peter's testimony in court might look like the following:

John:	Peter, would you please state your name for the court?
Simon Peter:	My name is Simon Barjonas. Some call me Peter.
John:	Peter, what can you tell us about Jesus? Who do you say he is?
Simon Peter:	I believe Jesus is the Messiah, the son of the living God. I believe there is no one else we can turn to for eternal life. He alone has the words of eternal life. I believe that he is the Holy One of God.

John: Peter, can you take us back to the Sunday morning after the crucifixion on Friday? Describe for the court what happened that Sunday morning.

Simon Peter: Sure. Several of us stayed in an undisclosed location behind locked doors. We feared what the authorities might do to us. They crucified Jesus. What would keep them from coming after us? So we hid. Anyway, on Sunday morning, someone pounded on our door. It was Mary, from Magdala. She told us that someone had taken the Lord's body from the tomb.

John: And what did you do next?

Simon Peter: Well, we ran to the tomb. Thinking back on it, we were taking a risk running out in public like that, but we had to see for ourselves what Mary had seen.

John: What happened next?

Simon Peter: We got to the tomb, found it empty, the grave clothes lying folded neatly where the body had been.

John: You mean Jesus' body, right?

Simon Peter: That's right.

John: Okay, go on.

Simon Peter: We didn't know what to do. We had no idea who might have taken Jesus' body, let alone where they might have carried it. We knew it was dangerous for us to be seen in public. So, after a few minutes, we quickly retreated to the upper room where we had been hiding.

John: And you remained in that room for the rest of that morning and most of the afternoon, is that correct?

Simon Peter:	That is correct.
John:	Something happened that evening. What happened?
Simon Peter:	We were in the room, locked doors. All of a sudden, Jesus just appeared with us. He tried to calm us down. He said, "Peace be with you!" Then, he showed us his wounds. It was definitely Jesus. We were speechless! Shocked! Overjoyed!
John:	What happened next?
Simon Peter:	I think he must have realized how dumbfounded we were. A second time, he said, "Peace be with you!" Afterward, he told us he was sending us out to spread the news about his resurrection. He talked to us about the Holy Spirit, and then breathed the Spirit on us.
John:	So there was no doubt in your mind that this was Jesus?
Simon Peter:	Oh, absolutely no doubt!
John:	No further questions at this moment, your Honor, but the defense requests permission to return the witness to the stand, if need be.
Judge:	Permission granted. The prosecution may cross-examine the witness.
Prosecutor Shaytan Kakos:	Thank you, your Honor. Have you always gone by the name Peter?
Simon Peter:	No.
Prosecutor Shaytan Kakos:	Who gave you your nickname "Peter"?
Simon Peter:	Jesus nicknamed me Peter.
Prosecutor Shaytan Kakos:	Jesus gave you your nickname?
Simon Peter:	Yes, Jesus.
Prosecutor Shaytan Kakos:	Usually, people give nicknames to people with whom they are close. So I am assuming that the two of you were

close, for him to give you a nickname. Is that correct?

Simon Peter: Yes, we were, um, are.

Prosecutor Shaytan Kakos: If I am not mistaken, the name Peter means "a rock," is that correct?

Simon Peter: Yes, sir.

Prosecutor Shaytan Kakos: That's what I thought. If it is all the same to you, I would rather call you Mr. Simon Barjonas than Peter. Is that okay with you if I call you Mr. Simon Barjonas?

Simon Peter: I suppose so.

Prosecutor Shaytan Kakos: Very good then! Mr. Simon Barjonas, you are a disciple of Jesus of Nazareth, are you not?

Simon Peter: Yes, sir. Yes, I am.

Prosecutor Shaytan Kakos: Have you always answered that question so affirmatively?

Simon Peter: Pardon me?

Prosecutor Shaytan Kakos: I asked you if you have always answered the question—Are you a disciple of Jesus?—so affirmatively?

Simon Peter: Well, I…cannot say.

Prosecutor Shaytan Kakos: Cannot say or will not say, Mr. Simon Barjonas?

Simon Peter: Well, I suppose, I—

Prosecutor Shaytan Kakos: Do you recall where you were on the morning of Passover, April 7, in the sixteenth year of our Emperor Tiberius, Mr. Simon Barjonas?

Simon Peter: Well, that was after a long night, sir.

Prosecutor Shaytan Kakos: Let me narrow it down a bit for you, Mr. Simon Barjonas. Do you know a young woman, a servant girl, named, let me see, Lycia?

Simon Peter: No, I don't believe I do.

Prosecutor Shaytan Kakos:	Well, Lycia certainly knows you, Mr. Barjonas. She said she saw you outside the courtroom the night of Jesus' interrogation by a campfire. She asked you—
John:	Objection, your Honor. This is nothing more than hearsay!
Prosecutor Shaytan Kakos:	Your Honor, we have Lycia's sworn affidavit given to the authorities. Defense has a copy of it.
Judge:	Overruled. I will allow it.
Prosecutor Shaytan Kakos:	Thank you, your Honor. Mr. Barjonas, Lycia says she came up to you while you were warming by a fire outside the interrogation area. She asked you a question. Do you remember her now, Mr. Simon Barjonas?
Simon Peter:	I think I may remember her. Yes.
Prosecutor Shaytan Kakos:	Could you please tell the court what her question was, Mr. Barjonas?
Simon Peter:	I don't remember *exactly*.
Prosecutor Shaytan Kakos:	Maybe I can refresh your memory, Mr. Barjonas. According to her sworn affidavit, the question was 'You were not one of Jesus' disciples were you?' Do you remember now, Mr. Barjonas?
Simon Peter:	Yes, I think I do.
Prosecutor Shaytan Kakos:	And what was your answer to Lycia's question?
Simon Peter:	*(Peter mumbles something)*
Prosecutor Shaytan Kakos:	I'm sorry, Mr. Barjonas, I did not quite make out your answer.
Simon Peter:	I told her I was not.
Prosecutor Shaytan Kakos:	Not what, Mr. Simon Barjonas?
Simon Peter:	I told her that I was not a follower of Jesus.

Prosecutor Shaytan Kakos:	Oh! So you have *not* always answered that question so…affirmatively! Hmm…Mr. Simon Barjonas, how long have you been a disciple of Jesus?
Simon Peter:	Over three years.
Prosecutor Shaytan Kakos:	Mr. Barjonas, you are actually the leader of the group, are you not?
Simon Peter:	Well, I wouldn't say that, I—
Prosecutor Shaytan Kakos:	Is it not true that you are usually the spokesperson for the group, Mr. Simon Barjonas?
Simon Peter:	Well, yes, sir.
Prosecutor Shaytan Kakos:	Mr. Barjonas, can you tell us, please, what your occupation was before you became the leader of the disciples?
Simon Peter:	I was a fisherman.
Prosecutor Shaytan Kakos:	A fisherman. Have you had any formal religious education, Mr. Simon Barjonas?
Simon Peter:	No, sir. I have not.
Prosecutor Shaytan Kakos:	No theological education that would qualify you as a theologian or even as the spokesperson for a group of expert theologians?
Simon Peter:	No, sir.
Prosecutor Shaytan Kakos:	In fact, none of the twelve disciples chosen by this Nazarene have any formal theological education, do they, Mr. Barjonas?
Simon Peter:	No, sir. None of us.
Prosecutor Shaytan Kakos:	Kind of odd, don't you think, Mr. Barjonas? I mean, here you are, charged with turning the world upside down for God, and yet you have absolutely no formal religious or theological training.

Simon Peter:	I guess one could consider it odd.
Prosecutor Shaytan Kakos:	Mr. Barjonas, let's go back to the night when you met our friend, Lycia, and you denied to her that you were a follower of Jesus. Did anyone else see you while you warmed by the fire that night?
Simon Peter:	A few people, yes.
Prosecutor Shaytan Kakos:	Did anyone else ask you if you were acquainted with Jesus?
Simon Peter:	*(Hesitantly)* Yes.
Prosecutor Shaytan Kakos:	How many more people, Mr. Barjonas, four or five? How many?
Simon Peter:	Two. Two people, in addition to the woman, asked me about Jesus.
Prosecutor Shaytan Kakos:	So three people in all asked you if you were with Jesus?
Simon Peter:	Yes.
Prosecutor Shaytan Kakos:	And you answered all of them the same way you answered Lycia, did you not, Mr. Barjonas? You told all three of them that you were not with Jesus. In fact, you told them you did not even know Jesus, is that not correct, Mr. Barjonas?
Simon Peter:	Yes.
Prosecutor Shaytan Kakos:	Is it true that you even threw out a few choice curse words for those people, Mr. Barjonas?
Simon Peter:	Well, about that, I—
Prosecutor Shaytan Kakos:	My, my! How can one go from being the leader of a small, exclusive group of Jesus' holy rollers, to someone who will not even admit that he knows Jesus at all? Oh, you do not have to answer the question, Mr. Barjonas. It is obvious that Jesus did not turn out to be all he

	was cracked up to be. It is easy to deny you know someone like that!
Simon Peter:	No, that's not the way it was!
Prosecutor Shaytan Kakos:	By the way, Mr. Barjonas, have you heard any…roosters…lately? Thank you, Mr. Barjonas, no more questions for this witness.
John:	Your Honor, the defense has a few more questions for the witness.
Judge:	Granted.
John:	Thank you, your Honor. Peter, do you regret denying Jesus?
Simon Peter:	Yes, I do.
John:	Did you later reconcile with Jesus?
Simon Peter:	I did reconcile with him.
John:	Will you please tell the court how that reconciliation came about?
Simon Peter:	Several of us had returned to our nets, fishing on the Sea of Galilee. We had caught nothing. From the shore, we heard someone shouting. We didn't know it at the time, but it was Jesus calling out to us. He told us to hoist our nets to the other side of the boat, which we did. And immediately, we started taking in more fish than we were able to handle. It was then that I realized who the stranger on the shore was.
John:	What happened next?
Simon Peter:	I jumped out of the boat, and helped the others haul the fish to the shore. Jesus had cooked breakfast on a campfire. So we ate.
John:	Okay. Then what?
Simon Peter:	After we ate, I kind of wandered a few feet away. It was still uncomfortable for me. I still felt the sting of my

denials. I could not face myself, let alone face Jesus.

John: But Jesus approached you, correct?

Simon Peter: He did. He came up to me and asked me if I loved him more than anything. And I did. I do! But I was in too much pain to say that I loved him enough to sacrifice everything for him. So I told him that I felt for him as though he was my brother. Then he told me to feed his lambs.

John: Is that how the conversation ended?

Simon Peter: No. He asked me a second time whether I loved him more than anything. I wanted to say that I did, but again, I just did not want to repeat the same mistake I had made before. I could not do that!

John: And what mistake was that?

Simon Peter: The mistake of promising something I could not deliver. I responded that I have a brotherly affection for him. Once again, he told me to take care of his sheep. Then he came back with a slightly different question. He asked if my feelings for him were like the feelings I would have for a brother. It hurt me that he kept asking about how I felt toward him. It also hurt me that he felt he had to come down to my level. But I answered him that I did feel for him like a brother.

John: And what did Jesus say?

Simon Peter: Again, he told me to take care of his sheep. He also mentioned that, at some future time, I would indeed show my love for him by giving my life for him.

John:	How did this conversation make you feel?
Simon Peter:	In the end, I was relieved. I knew that he had forgiven me, and I knew there was hope that my love for him would grow deeper.
John:	And Peter, again, who do you believe Jesus is?
Simon Peter:	He is the Christ, the Son of the living God! As I said before, I believe there is no one else we can turn to for eternal life. He alone has the words of eternal life. I believe and know he is the Holy One of God.
John:	Thank you. No further questions for the witness, your Honor.
Judge:	The witness may step down.

Mary Magdalene testified that she saw the risen Jesus. (John 20)

Mary Magdalene appears only a few times in the Bible, always in the Gospels, and mostly during the days surrounding the resurrection weekend. She is first mentioned in Luke 8:1-3 as one of the followers of Jesus named Mary, called Magdalene, meaning she was from the Galilean town of Magdala, about one hundred miles north of Jerusalem. In the same passage, Luke said that Jesus had cast seven demons from her. After the exorcism, she became a devout follower of Jesus. Mary was one of many women who accompanied Jesus during his travels, most of whom are believed to have been wealthy.

> After this, Jesus traveled about from one town and village to another, proclaiming the good news of the kingdom of God. The Twelve were with him, and also some women who had been cured of evil spirits and diseases: Mary (called Magdalene) from whom seven demons had come out; Joanna the wife of Chuza, the manager of Herod's household; Susanna; and many others. These women were helping to support them out of their own means.[220]

---

[220] Luke 8:1-3

At Jesus' trial and crucifixion, when most of Jesus' disciples abandoned him, Mary Magdalene was one of the women who stayed with him. She was present at the tomb, the first person to whom Jesus appeared after his resurrection, and the first person to spread the good news that Jesus had risen.

In the sixth century, confusion arose over the identities of Mary Magdalene, Mary, the sister of Martha, and an unnamed sinful woman from the Gospel of Luke (Luke 7:36-50). Both Mary, Martha's sister, and Luke's unnamed woman washed Jesus' feet with their hair. In the year 591, Pope Gregory the Great declared in a sermon that these three women were actually the same person, Mary Magdalene, and that Mary Magdalene was a prostitute. This view held sway until the Second Vatican Council, which, after much debate, declared the women to be three different persons and removed the prostitute label in 1969. Mary Magdalene is mentioned in each of the four Gospels, but not once do any of them mention that she was a prostitute.

After Jesus' death, the mystery surrounding Mary Magdalene's life would unfold. While she was the first to witness Jesus after his resurrection, nothing is known about where Mary went and what she did after Jesus' resurrection. One of the most extreme stories is that Mary, pregnant with Jesus' child, went to France, where her descendants eventually founded the Merovingian line of kings, made famous by Dan Brown's *The Da Vinci Code*. Brown's book depicts Mary as the Holy Grail in Da Vinci's The Last Supper, rather than the chalice from which Jesus drank. Brown's work was highly influenced by the book *Holy Blood, Holy Grail*, by Michael Baigent, Richard Leigh and Henry Lincoln. Some believe that Mary Magdalene and Jesus were married, but no evidence supports such a claim.

Western Catholics believe Mary fled in a boat with Lazarus and others to France where she lived in a cave for 30 years before dying at the Chapel of Saint Maximin, located about 75 miles northeast of Marseille, in southeastern France. In the Eastern traditions, Mary is believed to have left Jerusalem with Mary, mother of Jesus, and traveled to modern-day Turkey.

What is known for certain is that Mary Magdalene was a diligent follower of Jesus and the first to witness his resurrection.

> Early on the first day of the week, while it was still dark, Mary Magdalene went to the tomb and saw that the stone had been removed from the entrance. So she came running to Simon Peter and the other disciple, the one Jesus loved, and said,

> *"They have taken the Lord out of the tomb, and we don't know where they have put him!"*[221]
>
> Now Mary stood outside the tomb crying. As she wept, she bent over to look into the tomb and saw two angels in white, seated where Jesus' body had been, one at the head and the other at the foot.
>
> They asked her, "Woman, why are you crying?"
>
> *"They have taken my Lord away," she said, "and I don't know where they have put him."* At this, she turned around and saw Jesus standing there, but she did not realize that it was Jesus.
>
> He asked her, "Woman, why are you crying? Who is it you are looking for?"
>
> Thinking he was the gardener, she said, "Sir, if you have carried him away, tell me where you have put him, and I will get him."
>
> Jesus said to her, "Mary."
>
> She turned toward him and cried out in Aramaic, "*Rabboni!*" (which means "Teacher").
>
> Jesus said, "Do not hold on to me, for I have not yet ascended to the Father. Go instead to my brothers and tell them, 'I am ascending to my Father and your Father, to my God and your God.'"
>
> Mary Magdalene went to the disciples with the news: "*I have seen the Lord!*" And she told them that he had said these things to her.[222]

John's questioning of Mary Magdalene in his case for Jesus would not go into all the details of her life. Rather, John would ask her about how she came to know Jesus, and what she experienced at the crucifixion and resurrection. Mainly, John wanted to substantiate her belief that Jesus is the risen Messiah.

John:	State your name for the court.
Mary Magdalene:	My name is Mary.
John:	You are from the town of Magdala?
Mary Magdalene:	Yes.
John:	Do you know Jesus who is also called the Christ?

[221] John 20:1-2
[222] John 20:11-18

Mary Magdalene: I do. I followed him during his ministry. I still follow him today.

John: And what was your first acquaintance with Jesus?

Mary Magdalene: He cured me and some other women of evil spirits and disease.

John: After Jesus cured you, did you become one of Jesus' followers?

Mary Magdalene: Yes, I followed Jesus. Also, along with some of the other ladies, I supported Jesus financially.

John: Jesus had many followers. Some of them left him when he was arrested. What about you? What did you do after Jesus was arrested?

Mary Magdalene: I did not forsake him. I stayed with him, even at the crucifixion.

John: Who else was with you at the cross?

Mary Magdalene: Jesus' mother was there, along with his mother's sister, Mary the wife of Clopas, and you, of course!

John: Of course. Fast forward to Sunday morning, the morning you went to the tomb. You were among the first to arrive at the tomb, is that right?

Mary Magdalene: I *was* the first to arrive at the tomb.

John: Take us through what happened.

Mary Magdalene: I saw that the stone had been moved, and that the tomb was empty. The Lord was gone. I was shocked. I could not believe his body was gone. I immediately concluded that someone had moved Jesus' body. I ran to Peter and the other disciples. I told them that someone had taken the Lord out of the tomb, and we didn't know where they had put him!

John: What did Peter and the others do?

Mary Magdalene: Well, Peter and you, John, ran to the tomb. The two of you went inside, and found the grave as I had described it to you. Then you returned to the place where you all were staying.

John: Did you return with the disciples?

Mary Magdalene: No, I stayed at the tomb. Honestly, I was at a loss as to what to do or where to go. I was crying. I paced back and forth. At one point, I bent over to look again into the tomb and, when I did, I saw two angels in white, seated where Jesus' body had been, one at the head and the other at the foot.

John: Did you know they were angels when you saw them?

Mary Magdalene: No. I thought they were men. I had never seen either of them before, but they looked like men to me.

John: Did they say anything to you?

Mary Magdalene: They asked me why I was crying. I told them that someone had taken my Lord away, and I did not know where they had put him. At that point, I turned around and saw Jesus standing there, but I did not realize that it was Jesus. I thought it was the gardener. He asked me why I was crying and what I was looking for. I said to him, "Sir, if you have carried him away, tell me where you have put him, and I will get him."

John: But this man was not the gardener. He was Jesus.

Mary Magdalene: That's right.

John: What did he say to you?

Mary Magdalene: He looked at me and said, "Mary."

John: He called you by name?

Mary Magdalene: He did. He said, "Mary." I knew immediately it was the Lord. His voice was unmistakable. I turned toward him and cried out, "Rabboni!" I was so overwhelmed and speechless!

John: What happened next?

Mary Magdalene: I wanted to hold him and not let him go! But Jesus told me not to touch him because he had not yet ascended to the Father. He instructed me to go to his brothers and tell them that he was ascending to his Father. So I went as fast as I could to the others and told them that I had seen the Lord.

John: His brothers?

Mary Magdalene: His disciples.

John: I see. Mary, tell us, please, who do you believe Jesus is?

Mary Magdalene: I believe and now know that he is the risen Lord!

John: No further questions. Thank you!

Judge: Does the prosecution have any questions for this witness?

Asst. Prosecutor Paula Ponera: Yes, your Honor, we do. Thank you. Mary Magdalene, you said earlier that you hail from the Galilean village of Magdala, is that right?

Mary Magdalene: That is correct.

Asst. Prosecutor Paula Ponera: Do you live there now?

Mary Magdalene: I beg your pardon?

Asst. Prosecutor Paula Ponera: I asked if you still live in Magdala.

Mary Magdalene: Well, no, not exactly.

Asst. Prosecutor Paula Ponera: No, you do not live in Magdala. The fact is that you no longer live there because you do not have a good reputation among the people there. Is that not right, Mary from Magdala?

John: Objection, your Honor. This witness is not on trial here!

Asst. Prosecutor Paula Ponera: Your Honor, I am simply asking a straightforward question that calls for a straightforward answer. This question is meant to help us get some bearings on the credibility of the testimony of this witness.

Judge: Sustained! Next question, counselor!

Asst. Prosecutor Paula Ponera: Mary, you were once possessed by demons, is that correct?

Mary Magdalene: Yes.

Asst. Prosecutor Paula Ponera: How many demons?

Mary Magdalene: Uh, um, seven, I think.

Asst. Prosecutor Paula Ponera: How long were you under the influence of these demons?

Mary Magdalene: Several years, I do not know exactly how many.

Asst. Prosecutor Paula Ponera: When you were under the domination of these demons, how did you act? Were you erratic? Did you have convulsions? Give us some sense of what you were like.

Mary Magdalene: It was terrible. I had no control over my actions. My behavior was unpredictable, my body would at times convulse. I had seizures.

Asst. Prosecutor Paula Ponera: Did you have hallucinations? See unusual things?

Mary Magdalene: I may have. People said I did. I do not remember. Most of the time, I was unaware of what I was doing.

Asst. Prosecutor Paula Ponera: I see. How did people react to you when you were possessed by these many demons?

Mary Magdalene: They mainly just stayed clear of me. I think they were afraid. They did not know what to make of it.

Asst. Prosecutor Paula Ponera: Mary, under the influence of these demons, did you find that people tended to not take you seriously because of your being possessed by so many demons?

Mary Magdalene: Yes, sometimes.

Asst. Prosecutor Paula Ponera: You testified that, on the day Jesus supposedly came back from the dead, you saw angels at Jesus' tomb, but they first appeared to be men; and then you saw a gardener whom you did not recognize until you heard his voice. Then you said he was Jesus. Is this correct?

Mary Magdalene: Yes, it is.

Asst. Prosecutor Paula Ponera: When you went to tell Simon Barjonas and the other disciples about what you saw, they did not believe you, did they?

Mary Magdalene: No, not at first. But—

Asst. Prosecutor Paula Ponera: In fact, your words seemed like nonsense to them, is that not correct, Mary?

Mary Magdalene: Well, uh, yes, to begin with, but—

Asst. Prosecutor Paula Ponera: You just have a hard time getting people to believe you, do you not?

John: Objection, your Honor!

Asst. Prosecutor Paula Ponera: It must be really hard to live your whole life without anyone believing a word you say!

John: Honestly, your Honor! Objection! This witness is not on trial!

Judge: Miss Ponera!

Asst. Prosecutor Paula Ponera: No further questions, your Honor.

Thomas testified to having seen the resurrected Jesus. (John 20)

Thomas was a member of Jesus' inner circle of twelve disciples. Thomas appears first in John chapter 11 just after the death of their friend Lazarus of Bethany. Jesus decided to go to Bethany against the wishes of the disciples who remembered that certain Jews had attempted to stone Jesus in Judea. In John 11:16, Thomas sarcastically revealed his reluctance to go to Judea.

> Then Thomas (also known as Didymus) said to the rest of the disciples, *"Let us also go, that we may die with him."*[223]

We see Thomas again in John 14 where Jesus was preparing his disciples for his death. Jesus sought to assure the group that he would be going away to prepare a place for them, and that he would return for them. Then he made an obscure statement about the disciples knowing where he was going. Thomas responded, *"Lord, we don't know where you are going, so how can we know the way?"*[224]

Finally, we see Thomas in John 20 after Jesus had risen from the dead. Jesus first appeared to the disciples at a time when Thomas was not present. When the rest of the disciples told Thomas that they had seen Jesus, Thomas responded with skepticism.

> Now Thomas (called Didymus), one of the Twelve, was not with the disciples when Jesus came. So the other disciples told him, "We have seen the Lord!"
>
> But he said to them, *"Unless I see the nail marks in his hands and put my finger where the nails were, and put my hand into his side, I will not believe it."*
>
> A week later his disciples were in the house again, and Thomas was with them. Though the doors were locked, Jesus came and stood among them and said, "Peace be with you!" Then he said to Thomas, "Put your finger here; see my hands. Reach out your hand and put it into my side. Stop doubting and believe."
>
> Thomas said to him, *"My Lord and my God!"*[225]

[223] John 11:16
[224] John 14:5
[225] John 20:24-28

Throughout Christian history, Thomas has been caricatured for his doubt, thus earning the nickname "Doubting Thomas." While doubt can destroy one's faith, it can also strengthen a person's faith. Thomas' questions ultimately led him to a deeper faith. Thomas' testimony follows, beginning with the prosecution's questioning.

Prosecutor Shaytan Kakos:	Your name, please?
Thomas:	Thomas, also called Didymus.
Prosecutor Shaytan Kakos:	Thomas, you are a follower of Jesus, is that right?
Thomas:	I am.
Prosecutor Shaytan Kakos:	You are a follower of Jesus, but you were frequently skeptical of Jesus' plans, were you not?
Thomas:	Well, I wouldn't call it skeptical. It's just that I was—
Prosecutor Shaytan Kakos:	You would not call it skeptical? Is it not true that you disagreed with Jesus on a number of occasions? For instance, Mr. Thomas, do you remember where you were when you heard that your friend Lazarus was sick?
Thomas:	Uh, yes, we were in Galilee.
Prosecutor Shaytan Kakos:	Jesus did not leave immediately to be by his friend's side, did he? Even though the sickness was serious, even fatal?
Thomas:	Yes, that is correct.
Prosecutor Shaytan Kakos:	In fact, is it not true that Jesus did not go to Bethany until after Lazarus had been dead, let's see, four days?
Thomas:	Yes, that is true.
Prosecutor Shaytan Kakos:	Jesus was not around to visit his friend Lazarus in the hospital, and Jesus did not attend Lazarus' funeral. Is that not correct, Thomas?
Thomas:	Yes.

Prosecutor Shaytan Kakos:	*(Sarcastically)* Well! Well! What a friend we have in Jesus! Now when Jesus did finally decide to travel to Bethany, you were against going, were you not?
Thomas:	That is true. I was opposed to going to Bethany, but—
Prosecutor Shaytan Kakos:	In fact, none of Jesus' closest followers agreed with Jesus that going to Bethany was a wise decision, is that not correct?
Thomas:	Yes, that is correct. We were afraid of showing our faces near Jerusalem because the last time we were there, the authorities threatened our lives.
Prosecutor Shaytan Kakos:	Did Jesus listen to your objections?
Thomas:	Well, yes, he listened.
Prosecutor Shaytan Kakos:	But Jesus did not really listen to you, did he, Mr. Thomas? Jesus overruled your objections about going to Bethany, did he not?
Thomas:	Well, he—
Prosecutor Shaytan Kakos:	In fact, Jesus did not take your opinions into consideration at all, did he, Mr. Thomas?
Thomas:	I guess not.
Prosecutor Shaytan Kakos:	Do you recall the strange day when Jesus started talking about dying and going somewhere to prepare a place for his followers?
Thomas:	I do.
Prosecutor Shaytan Kakos:	Did you have any idea what Jesus was talking about?
Thomas:	Not at the time, no.
Prosecutor Shaytan Kakos:	What exactly did Jesus say that day?
Thomas:	He told us not to be troubled, but to trust in him. He told us that, in heaven, there are many dwelling places, and that he was leaving and

	going there to prepare a place for us. He said he would come back to take us there. He said that we knew where he was going and we knew how to get where he was going.
Prosecutor Shaytan Kakos:	But you did not know where Jesus was going, did you?
Thomas:	No. No, I didn't.
Prosecutor Shaytan Kakos:	In fact, you even told Jesus you did not know where he was going, did you not?
Thomas:	I did…tell him that.
Prosecutor Shaytan Kakos:	Wow! So Jesus said that you knew where he was going, but, in truth, you did not know. You had no idea where he was going! Jesus is not so all-knowing after all, is he? Hmm! Let's move ahead to the day Jesus was crucified. I am only guessing that, since you were a follower of Jesus, you were present with Jesus when he was being crucified? Is that right, Thomas?
Thomas:	No, I was not there.
Prosecutor Shaytan Kakos:	Oh, you were not with Jesus at his crucifixion? Well, then, what about the day Jesus supposedly rose from the dead? Mr. Thomas, were you among the disciples who went to Jesus' tomb that Sunday morning?
Thomas:	No, I was not.
Prosecutor Shaytan Kakos:	Were you present when the women came to report to the men that Jesus' body had been stolen?
Thomas:	No.
Prosecutor Shaytan Kakos:	No, in fact you were nowhere to be found! You were not around when Jesus was crucified; not around when

	he was in a tomb; and not around when the women came to report that Jesus' body had been stolen. The truth is, you were not around because you had long given up on Jesus being who he claimed he was, is that not true, Mr. Thomas?
Thomas:	No, that is not true!
Prosecutor Shaytan Kakos:	It most certainly *is* true, Mr. Thomas. Your actions speak louder than your words! You undoubtedly did not expect and did not believe that Jesus would come back from the dead, or you would surely have been around to see it, is that not true, Mr. Thomas?
Thomas:	Well, we did not know what to expect, just as we did not know what to expect when he walked into the temple, when he performed miracles, when he was teaching us. We couldn't quite grasp it, yet it was so clear.
Prosecutor Shaytan Kakos:	You still haven't answered my question, Mr. Thomas. Is it true that you did *not* expect Jesus to rise from the dead?
Thomas:	Well, I—
Prosecutor Shaytan Kakos:	Did you or did you not believe that Jesus would be raised from the dead, Mr. Thomas?
Thomas:	At the time, no.
Prosecutor Shaytan Kakos:	No what, Mr. Thomas?
Thomas:	No, I did not expect Jesus to be raised from the dead.
Prosecutor Shaytan Kakos:	And why did you not expect Jesus to come back from the dead?
Thomas:	I don't know. I just didn't.
Prosecutor Shaytan Kakos:	You do not really believe the myth that people can come back from the dead, do you, Mr. Thomas?

Thomas: Well, I—

Prosecutor Shaytan Kakos: When did you return to Jerusalem, Mr. Thomas?

Thomas: Later that same day, Sunday.

Prosecutor Shaytan Kakos: And when you returned, what did your friends say to you?

Thomas: They said they had seen the Lord.

Prosecutor Shaytan Kakos: They told you they had seen Jesus?

Thomas: Yes.

Prosecutor Shaytan Kakos: How did you respond?

Thomas: I told them that unless I could see the nail marks in his hands, put my finger where the nails were, and put my hand into his side, I would not believe it.

Prosecutor Shaytan Kakos: When your friends told you they had seen this dead man walking, you did not believe them, did you, Mr. Thomas?

Thomas: No, sir, I did not.

Prosecutor Shaytan Kakos: So, after having followed Jesus for over three years, and after having spent countless days, weeks, and months with others who followed him, you had seen enough to convince you that Jesus was no better than any other man, is that not right, Mr. Thomas? He could no more come back from death than any other man, is that not correct?

Thomas: But now I have seen enough!

Prosecutor Shaytan Kakos: But on that day, you did not believe it, did you?

Thomas: No, not on that day. But—

Prosecutor Shaytan Kakos: And rightly so, Mr. Thomas! Dead people do not walk, Mr. Thomas! Never have! Never will! No further questions, your Honor!

Judge: Defense's witness.

John: Thomas, you are the type person who must have things shown to him before he will believe them, right?

Thomas: I have to be convinced, yes.

John: Unless you see them, you do not believe them, yes?

Thomas: Yes, I guess so.

John: So, when Simon Peter and the women told you they had seen the Lord, you did not believe them.

Thomas: That's right.

John: So, did you ever see anything that convinced you that Jesus was alive, and that they truly had seen him?

Thomas: Yes, I did.

John: Tell us what happened.

Thomas: It was about a week later. We were still hiding out in Jerusalem. Behind locked doors. And suddenly, the Lord just appeared out of nowhere. Didn't open the door, a window, nothing! Just appeared! Though the doors were locked, Jesus came and stood with us. He said, "Peace be with you!"

John: Did Jesus say anything specifically to you, Thomas?

Thomas: Yes, he did. He turned to me, reached out his hands, and said, "Put your finger here; see my hands. Reach out your hand and put it into my side. Stop doubting and believe."

John: Was it truly Jesus who appeared to you that day?

Thomas: Oh! No doubt about it!

John: And what did you do?

Thomas: I looked at him, and said to him, "My Lord and my God!"

John:	"My Lord and my God!" That's what you said to him?
Thomas:	Yes.
John:	Did you reach out and touch his hands and his side?
Thomas:	Actually, no, I did not.
John:	Why not?
Thomas:	I didn't have to! I just knew it was the Lord! Seeing him, his presence, his voice…it was enough!
John:	Thomas, who do you believe Jesus of Nazareth is?
Thomas:	He is my Lord and my God!
John:	Nothing further. Thank you.

14 Closing Statements

The Prosecution's Closing Statement

The prosecution's closing statement will be delivered by the lead prosecutor, Mr. Shaytan Diablo Kakos.

Ladies and gentlemen of the jury…

I ask you again… *(Pointing to Jesus)* Does this man look like a god to you? That question is what this case is all about.

I want to thank you for your service in this trial, the case against Jesus of Nazareth, the so-called Christ. The time you have spent here hearing and considering evidence is of utmost importance.

As I said in my opening statement, this trial is not a trial about the existence of God. My team and I believe in God and such belief…

…makes us tremble. I am sure the same can be said for you all as well.

No, we are not here to argue the existence of God. Rather, this case is about a man who thinks he is God! The purpose of this trial is to argue whether this man, Jesus of Nazareth, is God! It is incumbent upon you, the jury, to decide if the defendant, Jesus, is in actuality who he claims he is, the Messiah, the Savior of the world…God! We, of course, do not believe that he is any of those things, and we believe we have presented enough evidence in this case to plant a sufficient doubt as to this man's claims about himself. The evidence has shown that, far from him being any Messiah or Savior, much less God, this Jesus is nothing more than a mere man. Any claims beyond these are not supported under closer scrutiny.

Serving on this jury comes with the responsibility that you take the evidence you have seen and heard, and render a decision without bias. I remind you that your verdict in this trial will affect not only the defendant in the case, but it will also impact you yourselves. For to believe that Jesus is Messiah, Savior, and God is to smack at the worst kind of idolatry, the kind of which would have shocked Moses and Abraham, leaving them turning over in their tombs! Would the one true God overlook such a twisted belief as what has been proposed by this defense? God will not because he cannot!

We have reached the conclusion of this trial. Therefore, now it is time for you to decide either for or against Jesus the so-called Christ. If you find the evidence to be compelling enough to decide against Jesus the Christ, then you must render a verdict that is against Jesus. Certainly, nothing that has been presented in this courtroom could lead us to believe that there is anything in this mere man that makes him worthy of our belief and trust.

The attorney representing Jesus of Nazareth has called witnesses, but everything they have said here has been easily refuted as subjective ramblings open to debate. There has been no evidence in their testimonies. Rather, mere hearsay!

The defense has presented what he calls physical evidence, but even this so-called physical evidence can be reframed in much more plausible ways than to suggest that this man Jesus was nothing more than, at most, a delusional illusionist skilled at sleight of hand.

The defense highlighted so-called prophecies, assigning to them meanings that the original authors of those statements would not dared have intended. Even our own esteemed religious scholars have said that these prophecies were not written to describe this man Jesus. The defense even purported to call God to testify, but did any of us actually see God come to the witness stand? Did you? Absolutely not! Rather, all we heard were statements that the defendant claimed to have heard God say, or that some of his blinded and brainwashed followers claimed to have heard God say. In most courts of law, this would have been declared hearsay and therefore would not have been allowed into evidence at all!

You see, ladies and gentlemen, the defense is desperate and weak! The defense attorney wanted to convince you that Jesus is the long-promised Messiah. But he has not succeeded! How could he succeed? If this man Jesus were truly the Messiah, truly God, truly the healer of terminal diseases, then why did he not travel to every hospital, every sick bed, for the sake of all humanity, and heal everyone who had an incurable disease? Indeed, why would he not? If he could truly raise the dead by simply waking them with his voice, then why did he not tour every cemetery throughout Palestine raising every deceased person from the dead? I am sure that you all have loved ones that you would love to see again, perhaps a mother or a father, or maybe a child, whom you would love to have seen raised from the dead, but did this alleged resurrectionist raise any of them from the dead? No. Why? Because he could not! And if he could raise your loved ones from the dead, but did not, then he is indeed the most calloused man to ever walk the face of the earth. Hardly worthy of being called God! If he were truly God, he would not need defending!

Why, Jesus' own followers and even his family members ended up forsaking him. Now, if his own family and closest followers ended up forsaking him when he needed them the most, what does this say to you and me?

For this and many other reasons, Miss Ponera, Mr. Skotia, and I are confident that you have found the arguments of the defense to be unpersuasive and without the slightest fragment of merit.

Ladies and gentlemen, we are here to determine the truth. And truth is that Jesus is not God. He is not the Christ. He is not the Savior of the world. In fact, he could not even save himself, let alone anyone else. Rather, he is nothing more than you or I, an ordinary human being.

You see, the defense has underestimated you. He does not believe you are intelligent. He is counting on your inability to see through the façade of divinity he has cloaked around this mere man, Jesus. He does not believe that this jury…

…is smart enough to reject Jesus' claim of lordship.

But I plead with you! Do not let him get away with insulting your intelligence in such a way!

In the interest of truth, I ask you now to decide against Jesus the so-called Christ. Let us put this matter to rest, once and for all. I assure you that, if you decide against this man this day, as you should, within a few months, no one will remember him, for the world's memory of him will fade into nothingness. You, however, will be remembered for having made the momentous decision that saved us all from perhaps our nation's most notorious imposter. You will be the ones to go down in history as having saved the world, not he. Thank you very much.

John's Closing Statement

Ladies and gentlemen…

I, John, stand before you today to declare that this Jesus, whom the prosecution wishes to dismiss as a mere man, is none other and nothing less than God in the flesh! He is the one and only Lamb of God who takes away the sin of the world!

Jesus was in the beginning, and Jesus was with God, and, contrary to what Mr. Shaytan Diablo Kakos would have you believe, Jesus was and still is God!

He was with God in the beginning. Through him all things were made; without him nothing was made that has been made. In him was life, and that life was the light of all humankind. The light shines in the darkness, and the darkness has not been able to overcome it.

In this trial, you have heard numerous witnesses who attest to his light and life. Among them was a man sent from God whose name is John the Baptizer. He came as a witness to testify concerning that light, so that through that light all might believe. John himself was not the light; he came only as a witness to the light. But John testified concerning him. He cried out, saying, "This is the one I spoke about when I said, 'He who comes after me has surpassed me because he was before me.'" I submit to you that Jesus Christ, the true light that gives light to everyone, was coming into the world. Jesus was in the world, and though the world was made through him, the world did not recognize him. He came to that which was his own, but his own did not receive him. Yet, to all who did receive him, to those who believed in his name, he gave the right to become children of God— children born not of natural descent, nor of human decision or a husband's will, but born of God. This is true for you who serve on this jury as well!

In Jesus, God became flesh and made his dwelling among us. Those of us who knew him have seen his glory, the glory of the one and only Son, who came from the Father, full of grace and truth. Out of his fullness we have all received grace in place of grace already given. For the law was given through Moses; grace and truth came through Jesus Christ. No one has ever seen God, but the one and only Son, who is himself God and is in closest relationship with the Father, has made him known. Furthermore, what God has made known in Jesus, we have seen through miraculous signs, of which I have highlighted only a few! Jesus performed many other signs in the presence of his disciples, which are not recorded in this trial. But we have presented these to you that you may believe that Jesus is the Messiah, the Son of God, and that by believing you may have life in his name.

Ladies and gentlemen of the jury, I too join you in the pursuit of truth. And the truth is that Jesus of Nazareth is the Christ, the Savior of the world, and he is God. I urge you to return to this courtroom with a verdict in favor of Jesus Christ. Thank you.

15 Time for the Jury to Decide

In the courtroom, after all the evidence has been presented, all the witnesses have testified, all the experts have been called in, and all the historical precedence has been cited, it comes down to the jury to make a decision. Many of those jury trials have been famous. Take for instance the jury trial of Henry Ward Beecher in 1875.

From 1850 to 1880, Henry Ward Beecher was the most popular Protestant minister in the United States, the Billy Graham of his time. Beecher's father was the famous Calvinist theologian Lyman Beecher, and his sister was Harriet Beecher Stowe, the author of best-selling novel *Uncle Tom's Cabin.* Henry Ward Beecher was a Congregationalist pastor, social reformer, prolific writer and speaker. As the first pastor of the Plymouth Church in Brooklyn, he received the highest salary of any clergyman at the time—$100,000 a year. He was known for his support of the abolition of slavery, his emphasis on God's love as opposed to full-blown Calvinism, and his 1875 adultery trial.

Beecher's former friend and protégé, journalist Theodore Tilton, accused Beecher of seducing Tilton's wife, Elizabeth. The Tiltons had been among Beecher's most faithful church members. Beecher had officiated the Tiltons' wedding. Together, Henry Ward Beecher and Theodore Tilton edited *The Independent*, one of the most influential religious periodicals in the country. However in 1870, Elizabeth Tilton confessed to her husband that she and Beecher had engaged in an extramarital relationship, though she later adamantly denied it. The charges became public when Theodore Tilton told feminist Elizabeth Cady Stanton of his wife's confession. Stanton repeated the story to fellow women's rights leaders Victoria

Woodhull and Isabella Beecher Hooker, who was also Beecher's sister. Woodhull was an advocate of free love, by which she meant the freedom to marry, divorce, and bear children without government interference. It was a position Henry Ward Beecher had publicly denounced. Outraged at what she construed as Beecher's hypocrisy, in November 1872, Woodhull published the story in her newspaper, *Woodhull and Claflin's Weekly*, under the title, "The Beecher-Tilton Scandal Case." The story ignited a firestorm in the national press. The scandal came to a boiling point in 1875 when Theodore Tilton sued Beecher in civil court on the charge of "criminal conversation," adultery, and for the "alienation of affections" of Tilton's wife. The trial lasted six months, after which time the case was handed over to the jury for deliberations. The jurors deliberated for six days without being able to reach a verdict. Three jurors voted against Beecher; nine jurors voted in his favor. The fact that the jurors could not reach a decision was a decision in itself. Tilton's charges were dismissed. The scandal split the Beecher siblings; Harriet and others supported Henry, while Isabella supported Woodhull. The American public also remained divided over Beecher's culpability, but the jurors, though divided, had made a decision.[226]

One of the longest jury deliberations ever occurred in 1992 in Long Beach, California. The lawsuit, filed by Shirley and Jason McClure, accused city officials of violating the U.S. Fair Housing Act by conspiring to prevent Mrs. McClure and her son Jason from opening a string of residential homes specifically designed for Alzheimer's patients in upscale Long Beach neighborhoods. The case took eleven years to get to trial and six months to get through courtroom testimonies. In all, the case lasted 209 days, consisted of 112 days of testimony, included the testimony of 90 witnesses, and examined 4,000 exhibits of evidence.

Once the case was turned over to the jury, the jury deliberated for 371 hours (four and a half months). During their deliberations, jurors often chatted, slept, read, and joked around instead of talking about the evidence. They frequently started deliberations late and ended early. And to give themselves a "mental break," one juror orchestrated a phony sick call to court so he and a few others on the panel could attend a horse race. In addition, several in the group drank alcohol with their lunches during the testimony portion of the trial. Later, when the court footed

[226]http://topics.nytimes.com/top/reference/timestopics/people/b/henry_ward_beecher/index.html

the lunch bills, some occasionally ordered more than they could eat and took the rest home. Three jurors became so chummy that they took weekend vacations together. Finally, the jury awarded Shirley McClure $20 million in damages and her son $2.5 million — a record for the city of Long Beach.[227] The jurors took their time, but ultimately they did make a decision.

By John's calendar, the courtroom trial of Jesus the Christ lasted approximately three and a half years, which was about the length of Jesus' ministry. This calculation is based on the fact that John described Jesus as making at least three, perhaps four, treks to Jerusalem during Passover, the last resulting in his crucifixion. John has done all he could do to convince the jury that Jesus is indeed the Christ. John has clearly stated his theme, crafted his opening and closing statements, called witnesses to testify, presented physical evidence, enlisted the help of an expert witness, relied on historical precedent, cross-examined prosecution witnesses, sought the wisdom of Israel's founders, and even took the bold step of bringing Jesus himself to testify. The trial ended by sending the case to the jury.

And you and I are on this jury.

In fact, juries have been deliberating Jesus' fate ever since John wrote his Gospel near the end of the first century. Every person who reads John's words becomes part of the jury with the inescapable responsibility of rendering a decision. But, more than determining the fate of Jesus, by making a decision, jurors determine their own fate. Our eternal futures hinge on what we decide about Jesus.

Now we may say, "I'm not making a decision about Jesus." But the decision not to make a decision is tantamount to making a decision. Juries have no choice but to decide, to render verdicts. And, as happens so often in court cases, the decisions jurors make impact those jurors for life.

So again, the trial is over. The deliberation has begun. You are on the jury.

What will you decide about Jesus?

---

[227] http://lang.presstelegram.com/projects/mcclure/

ABOUT THE AUTHOR

Jimmy F. Orr is the pastor of Palmetto Baptist Church, Palmetto, Georgia, where he has served since September 2000. Dr. Orr holds degrees from the University of Georgia and the New Orleans Baptist Theological Seminary. In addition to Palmetto Baptist Church, he has served Bethlehem Baptist Church and Concord Baptist Church, both in Cumming, Georgia. Since 2004, Dr. Orr has taught as an adjunct professor of Christian Studies at the Brewton-Parker College, Newnan, Georgia campus, and he also teaches at the Frederick M. Hawkins Center for Biblical Christian Studies, in Cumming, Georgia. Dr. Orr and his wife Amanda have two children, Zach (and his wife, Micole) and Hillary, and reside in Palmetto, Georgia.

Other Books by Dr. Jimmy F. Orr

The God Questions – The Questions God Asked in Scripture

Made in the USA
Middletown, DE
20 December 2015